THIS BOOK BELONGS TO :

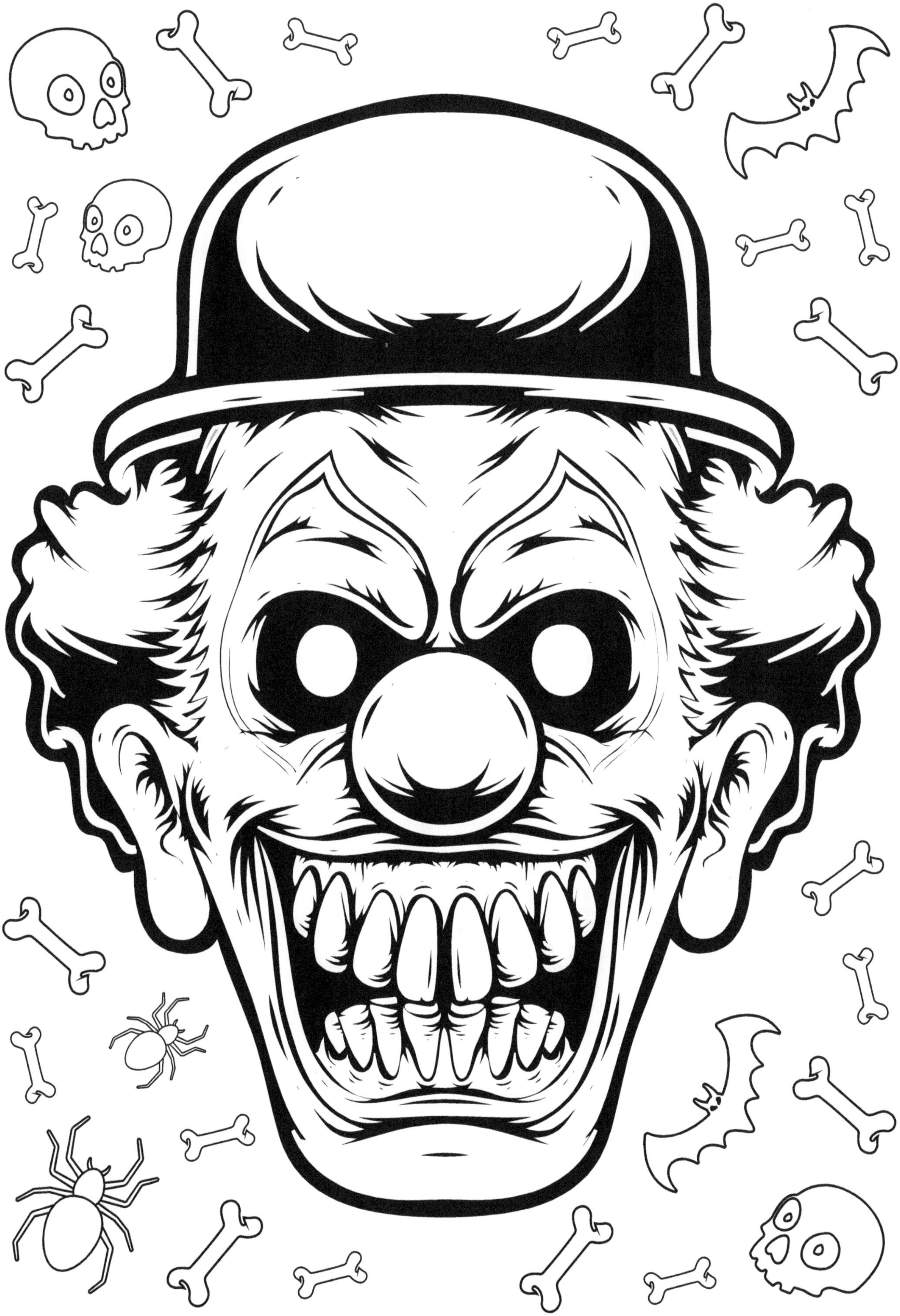

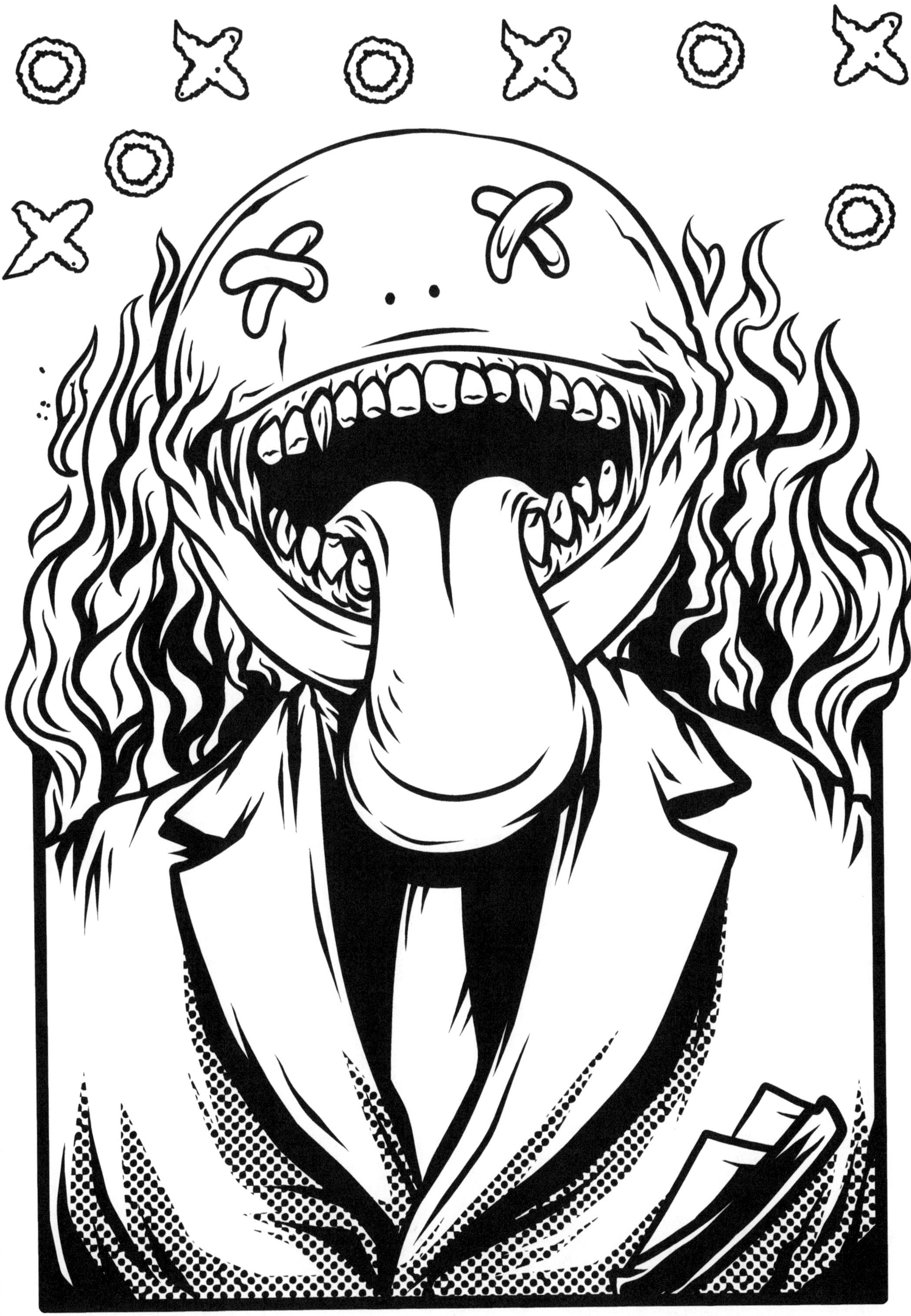

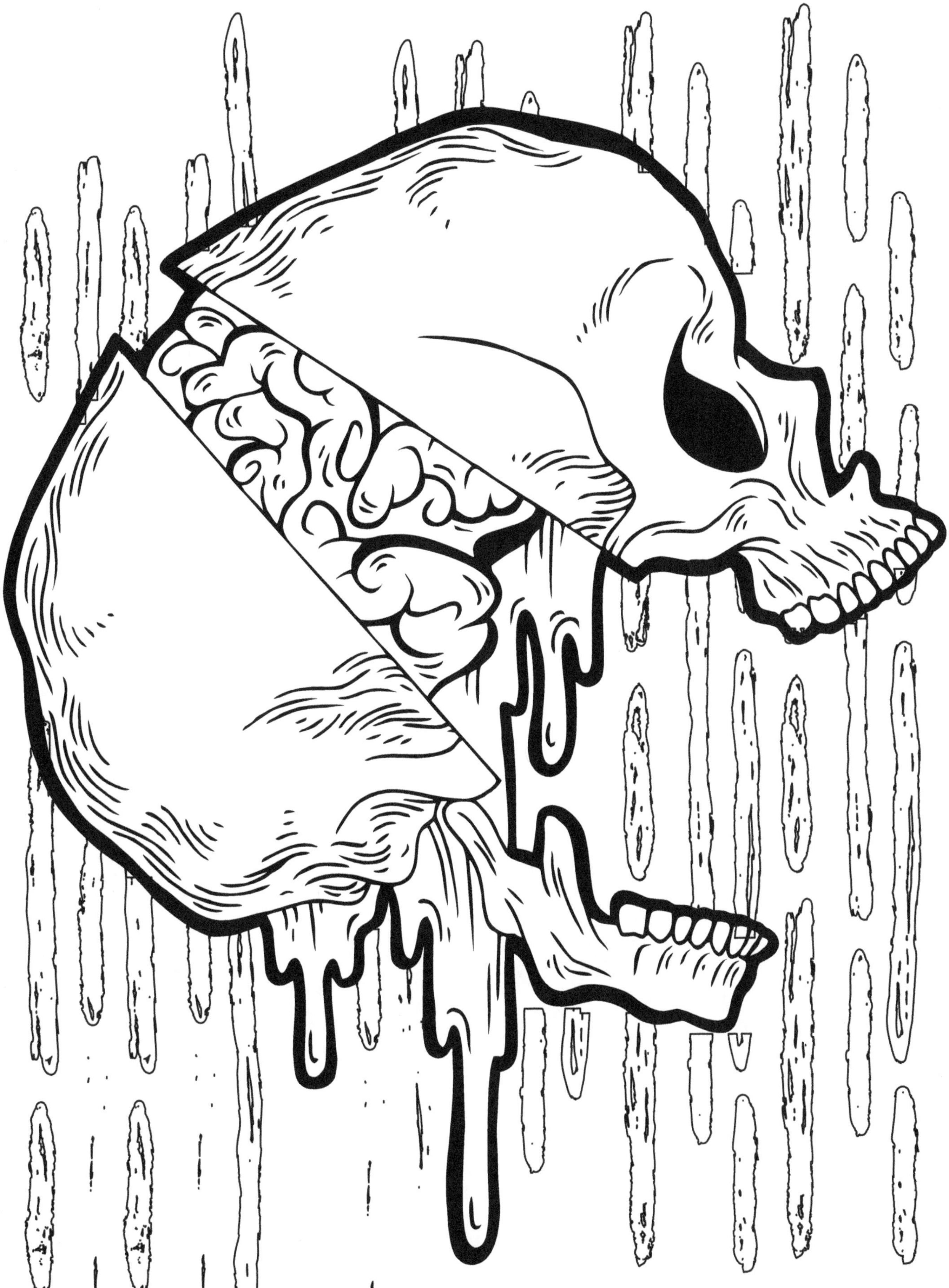

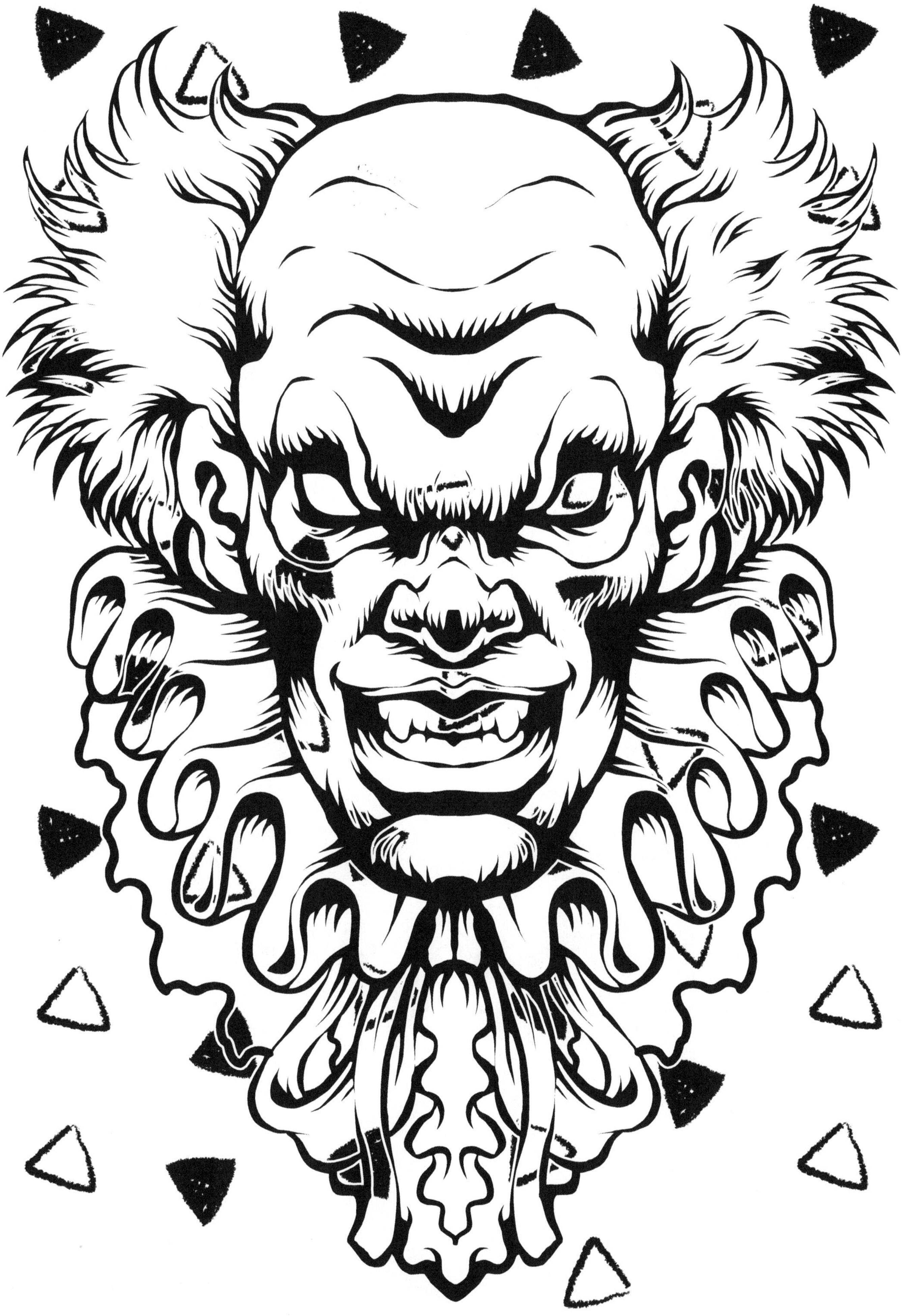

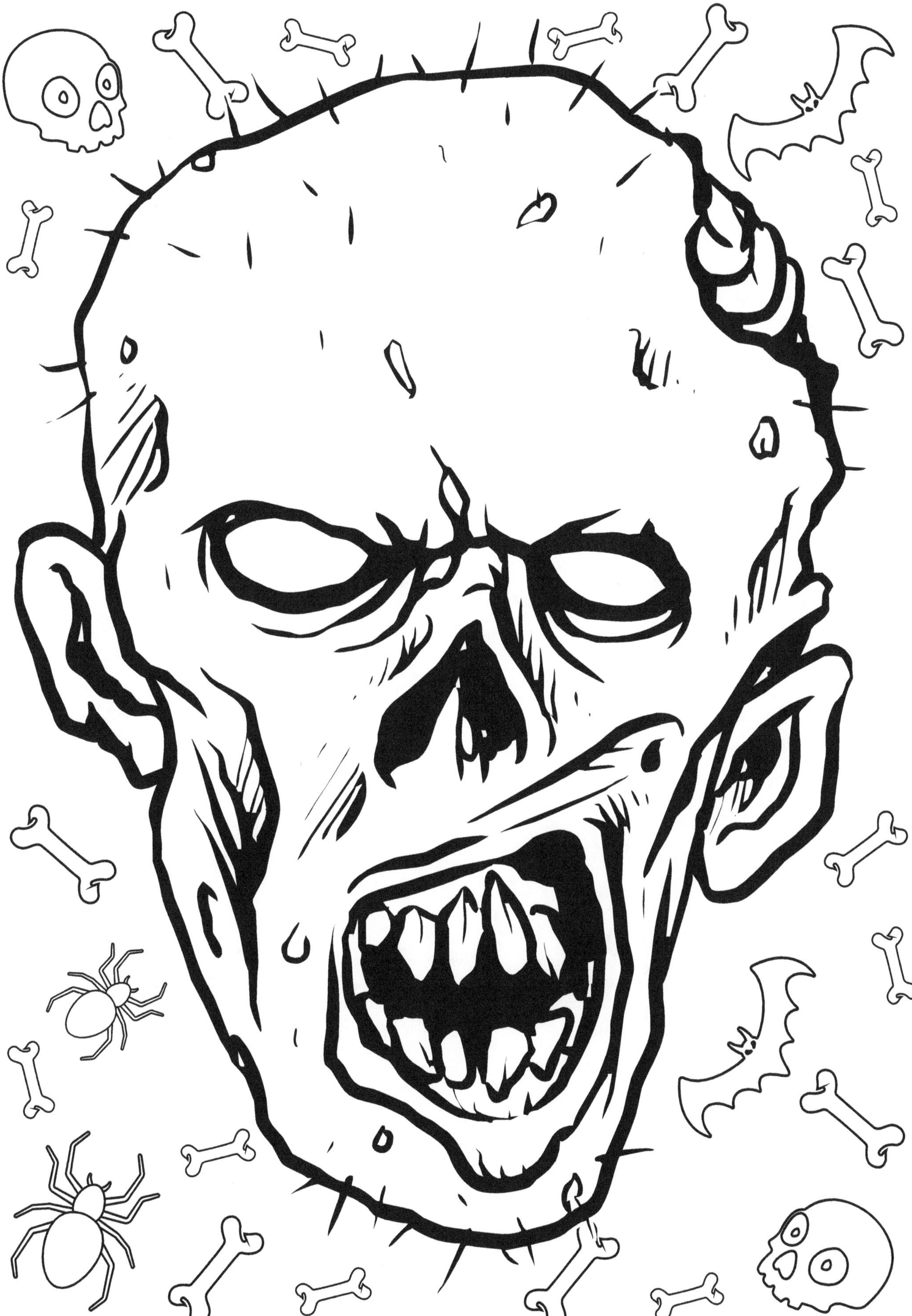

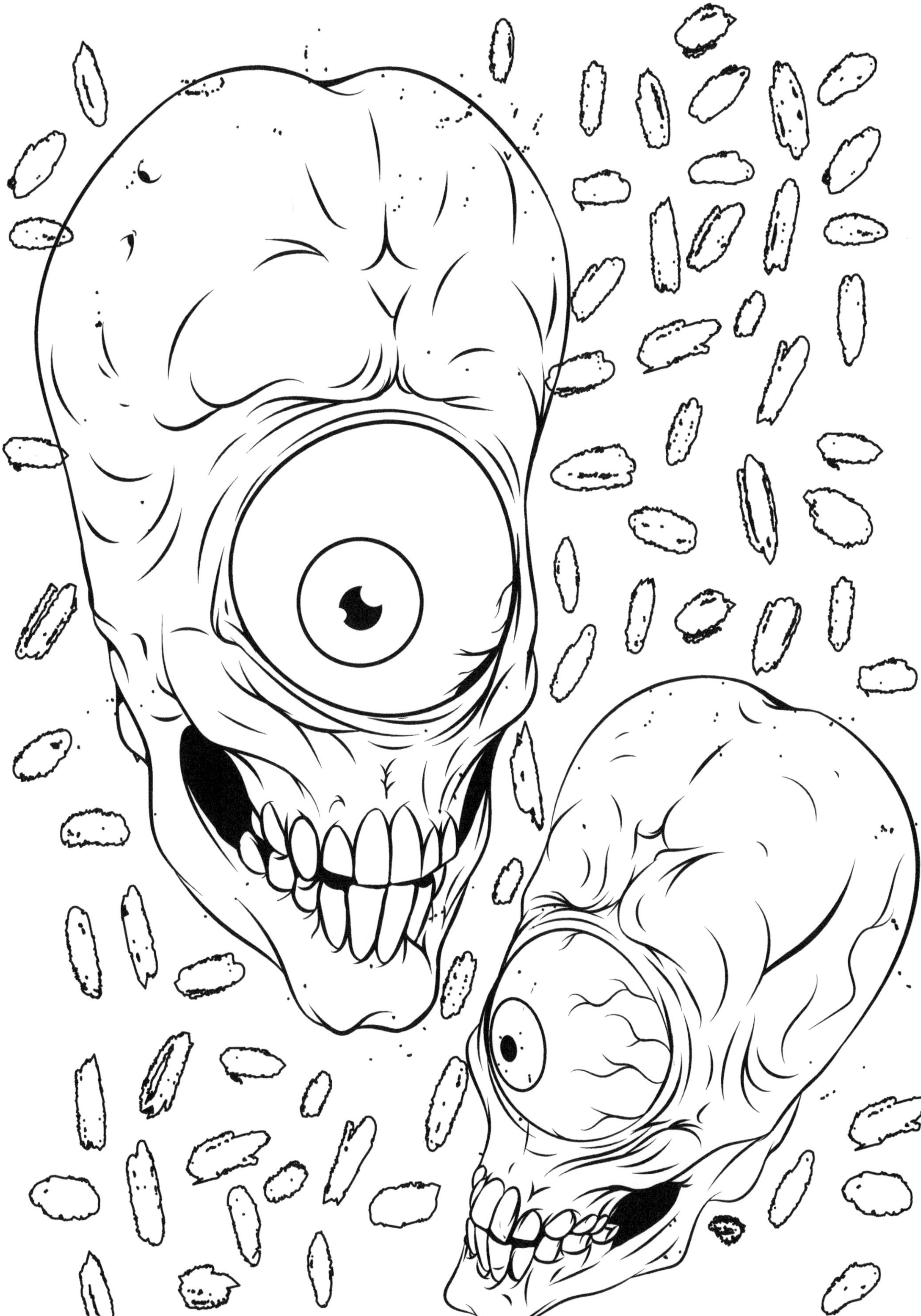

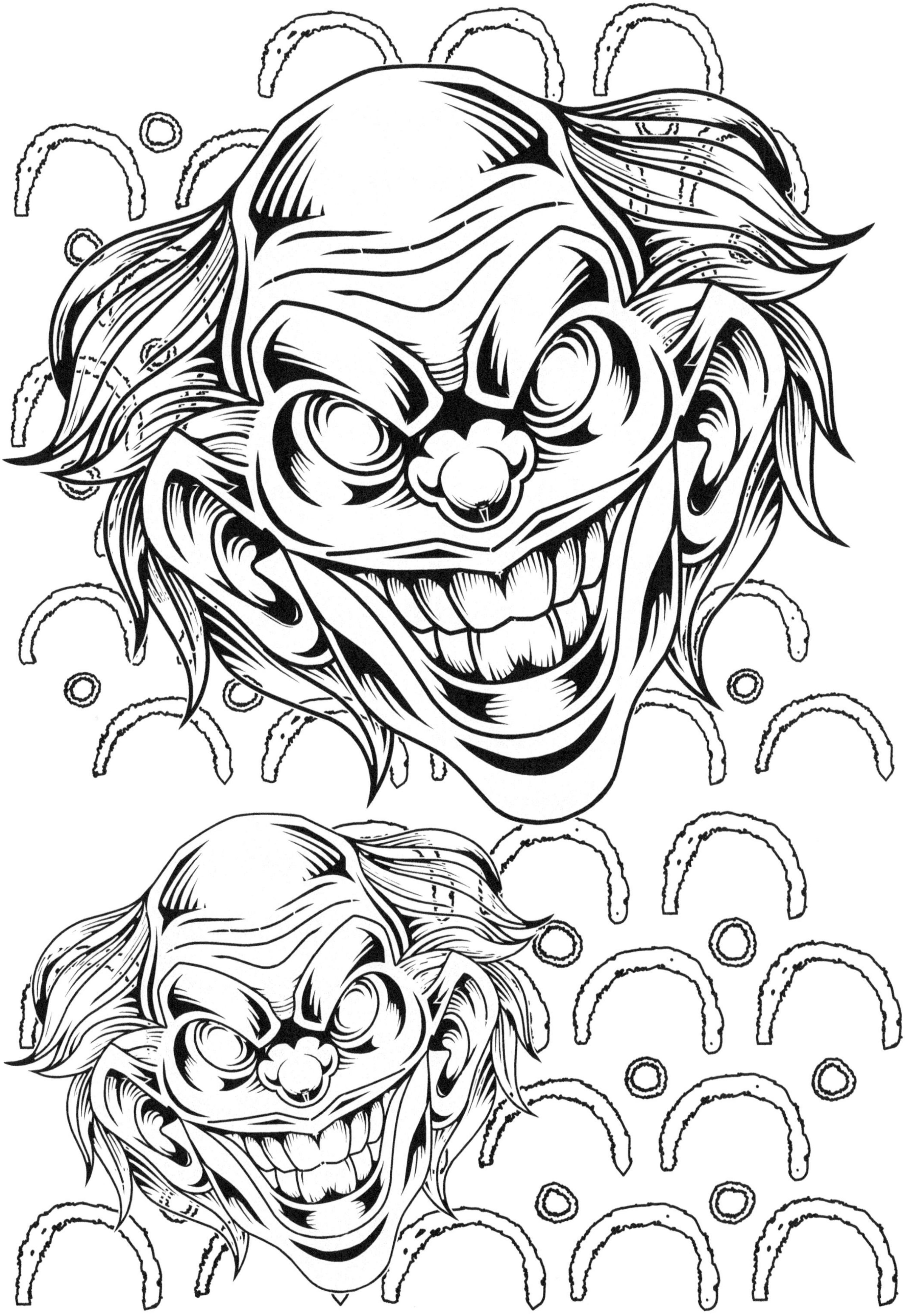

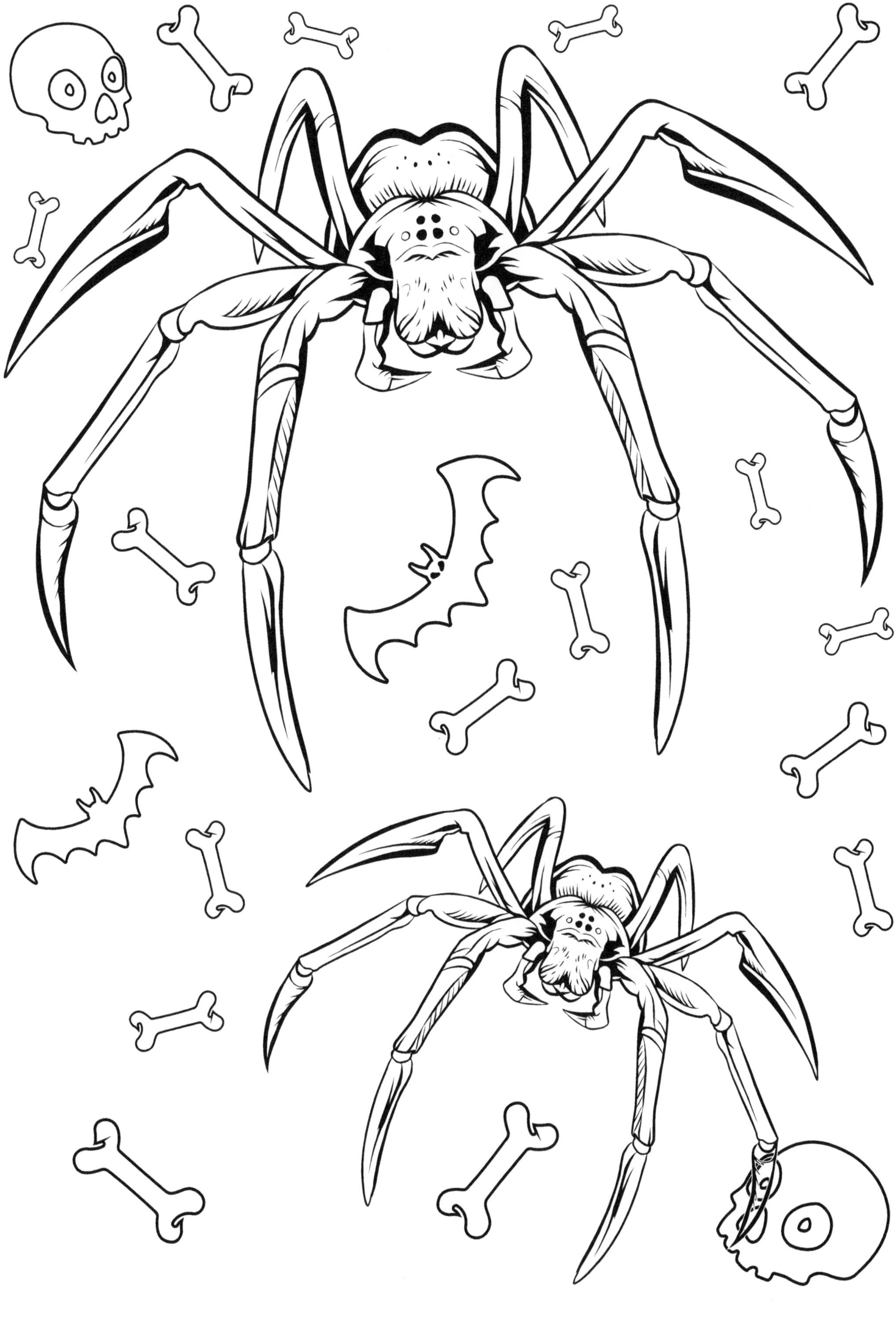

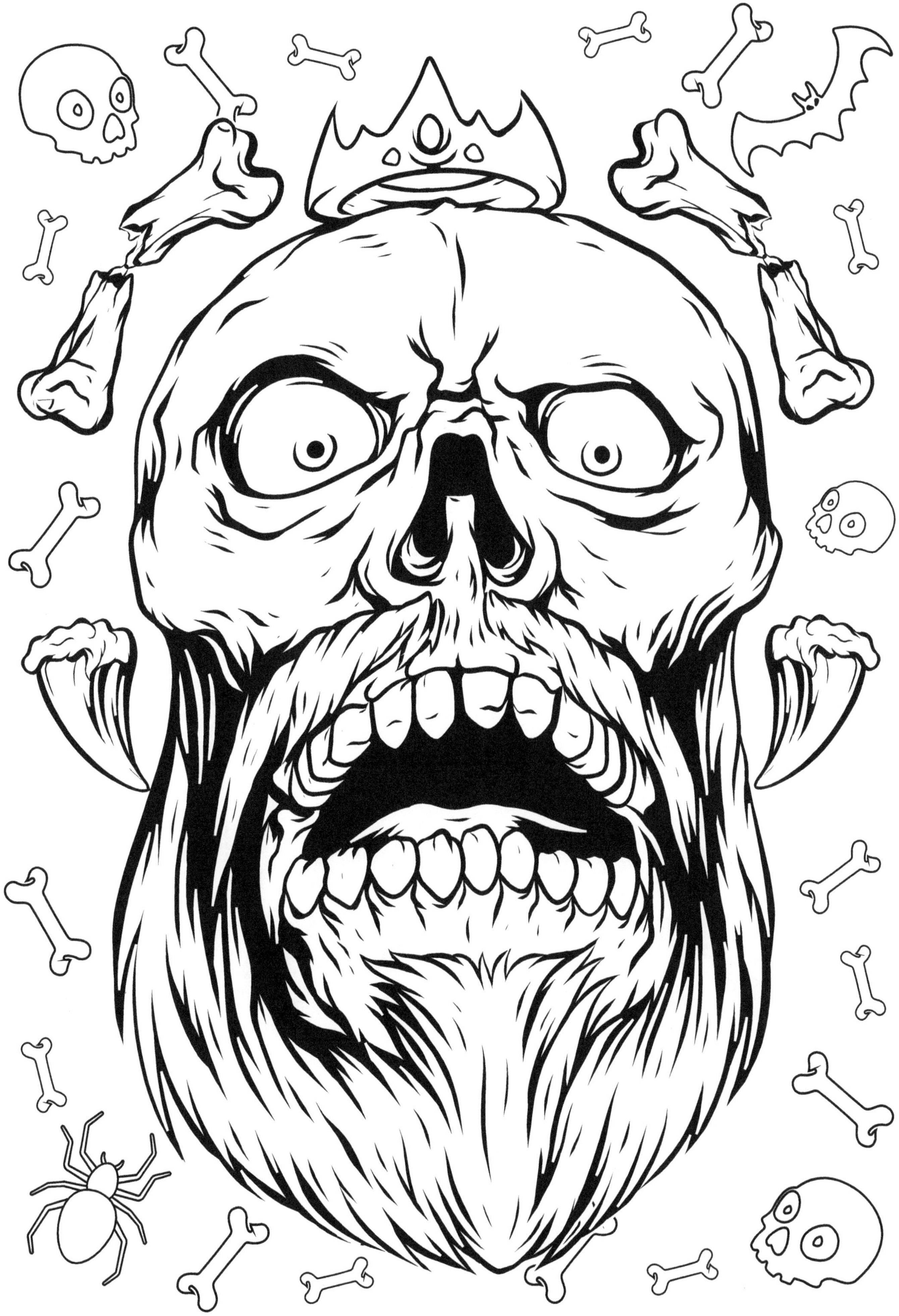

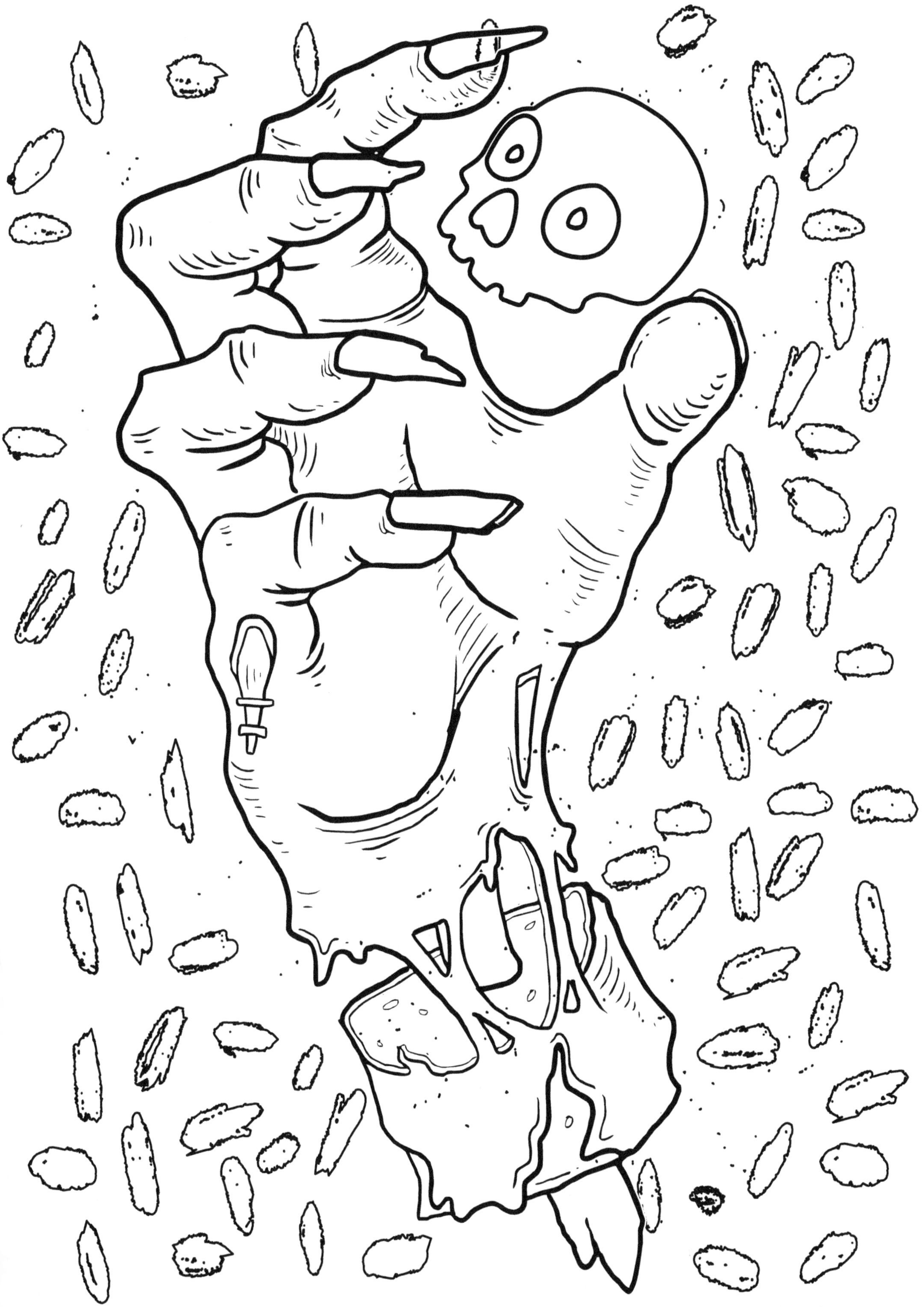

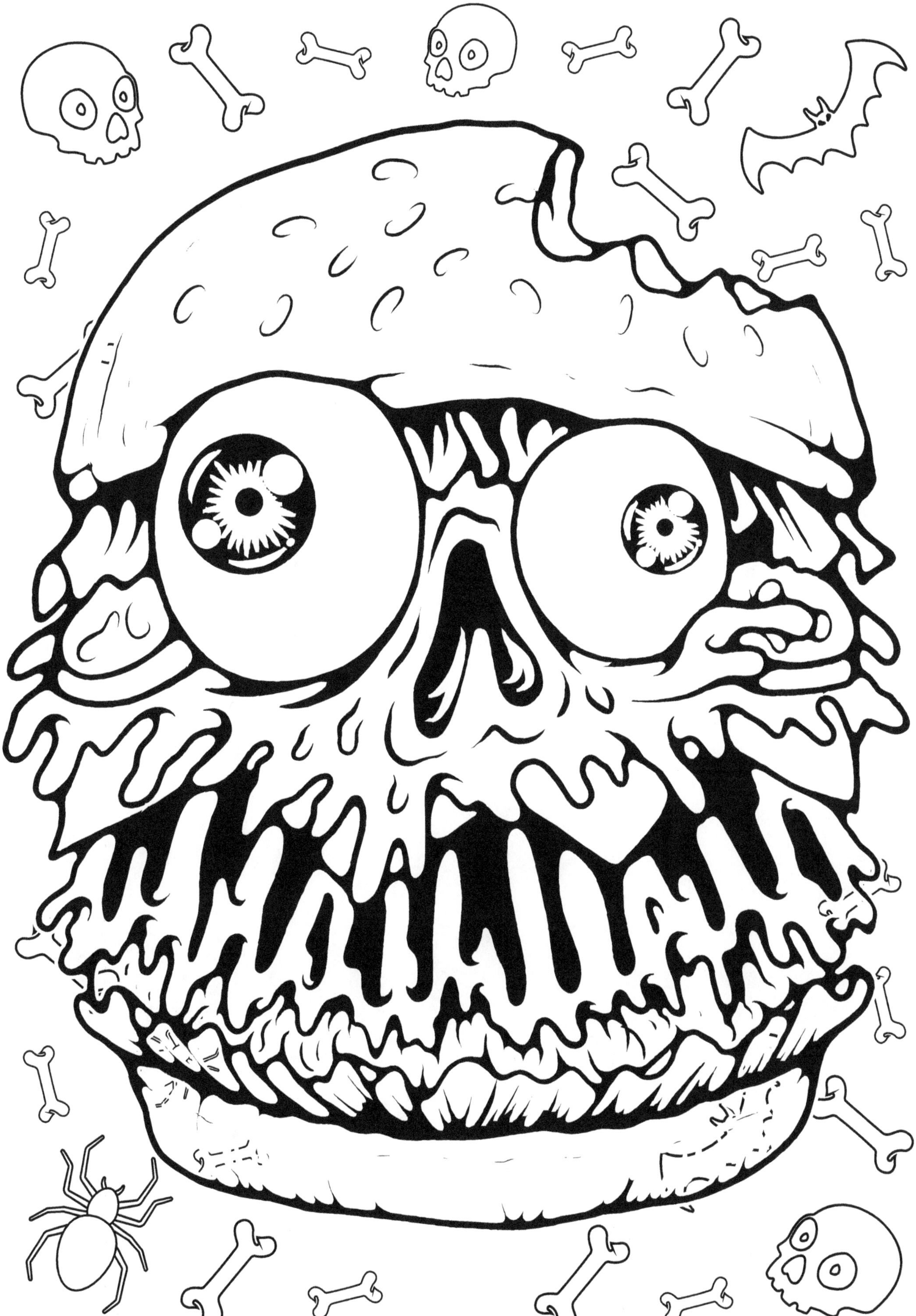

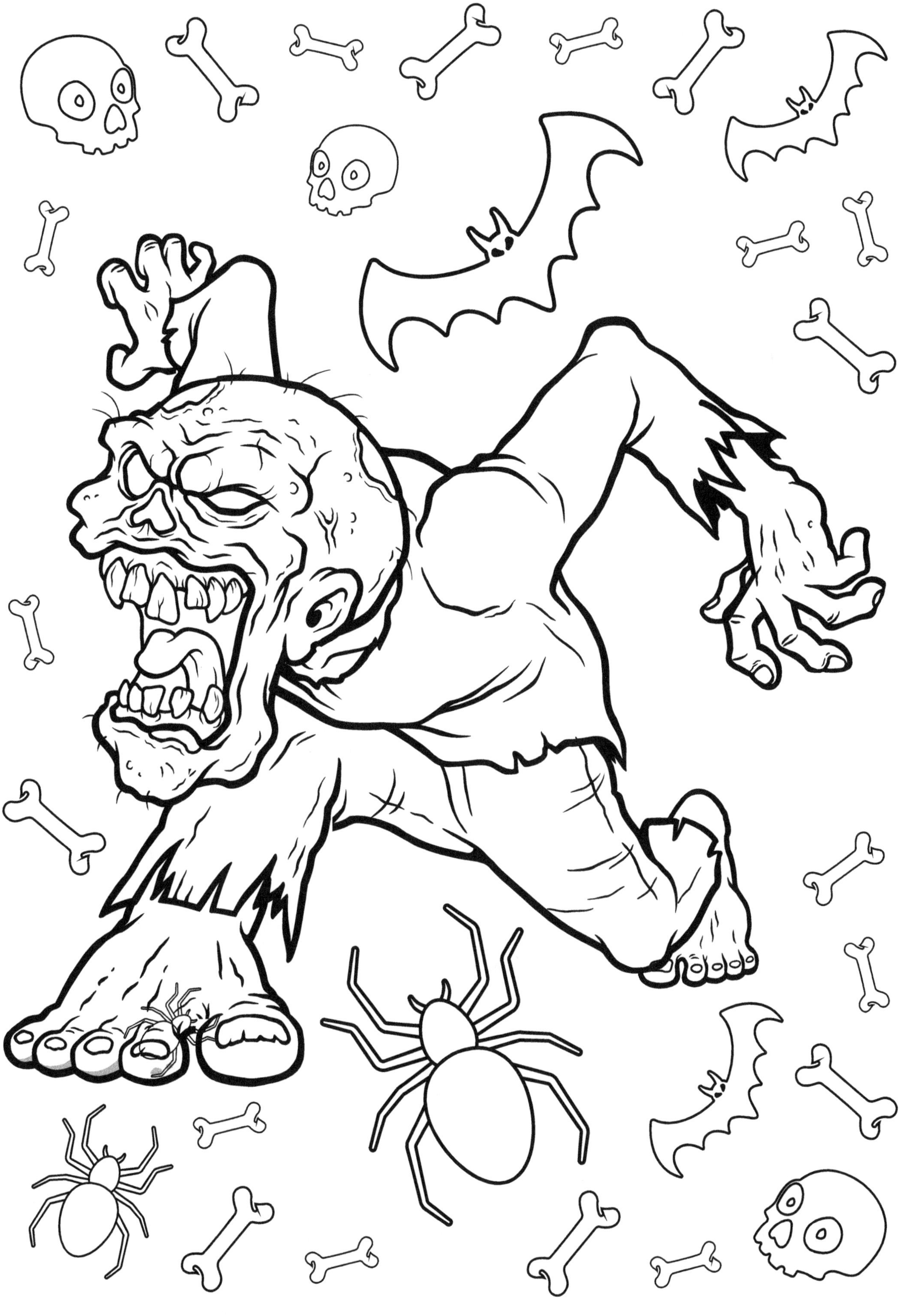

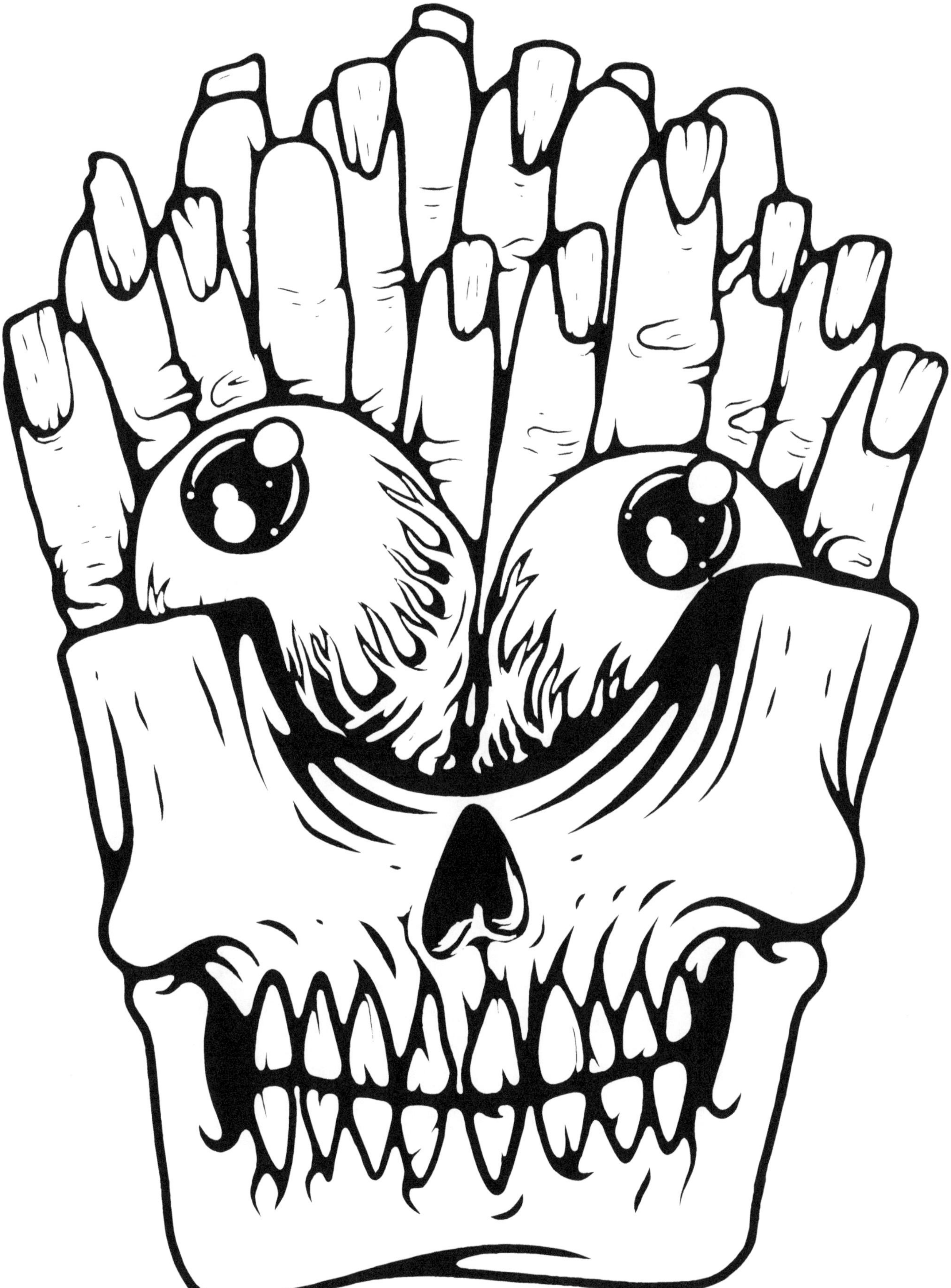

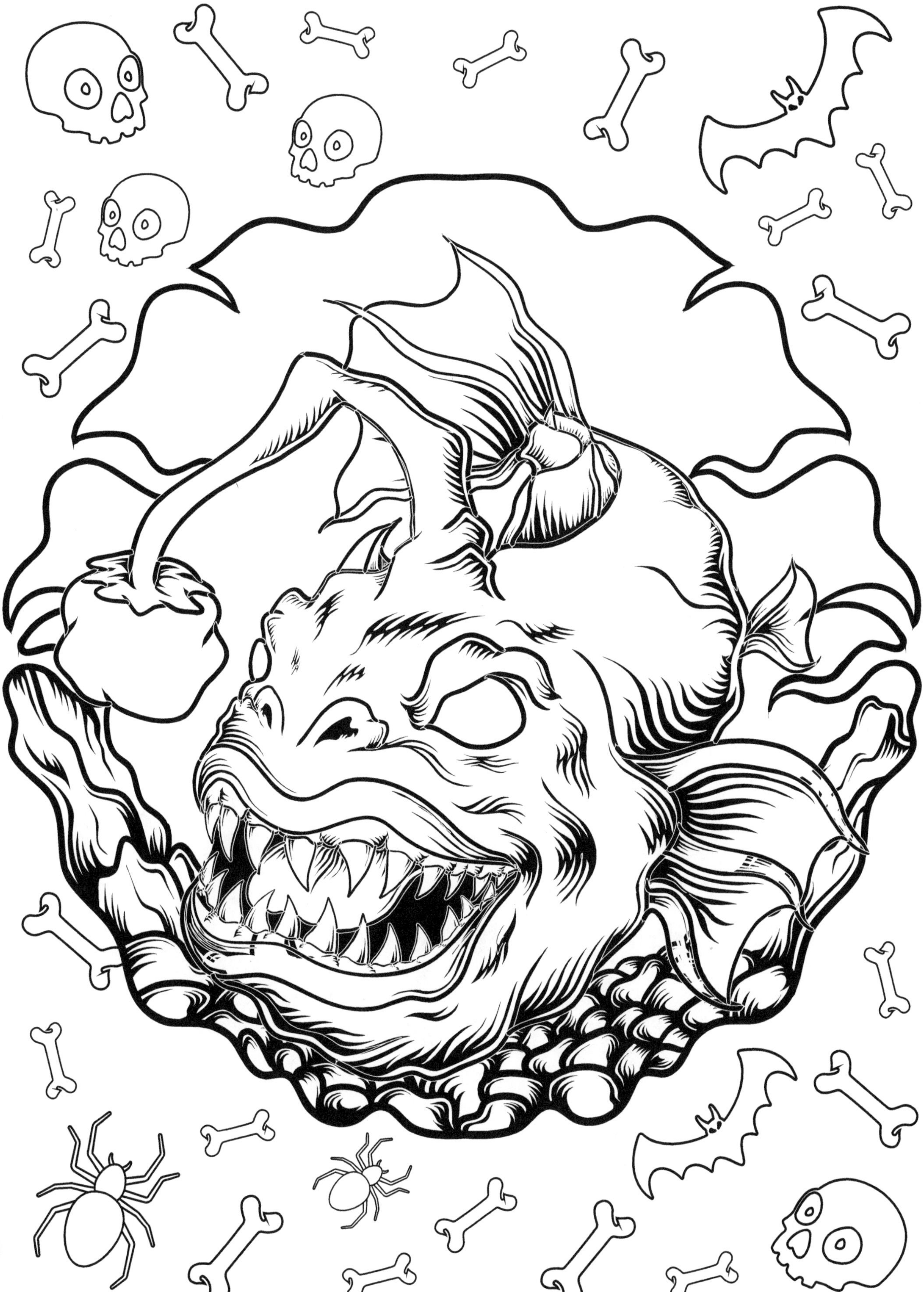

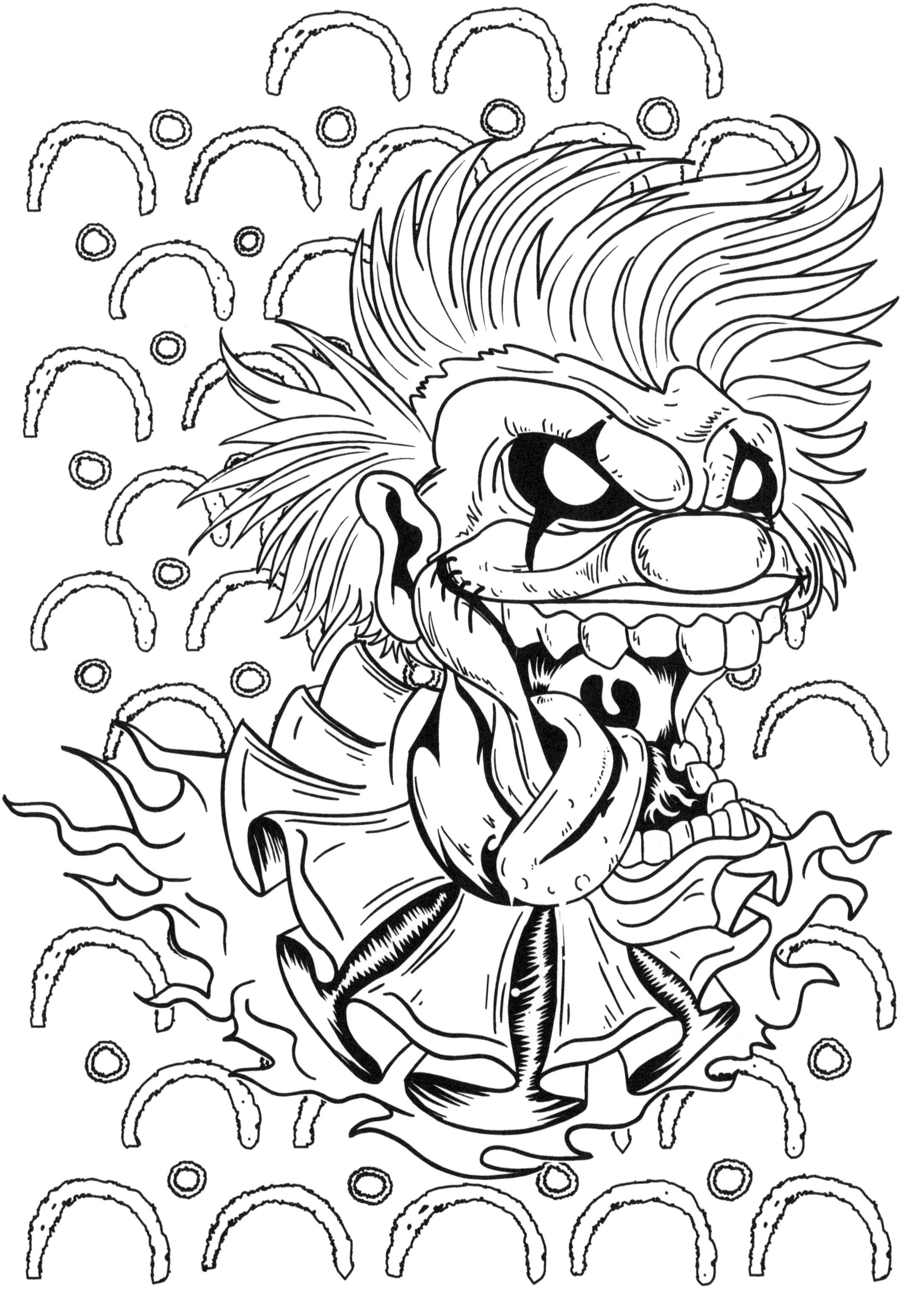

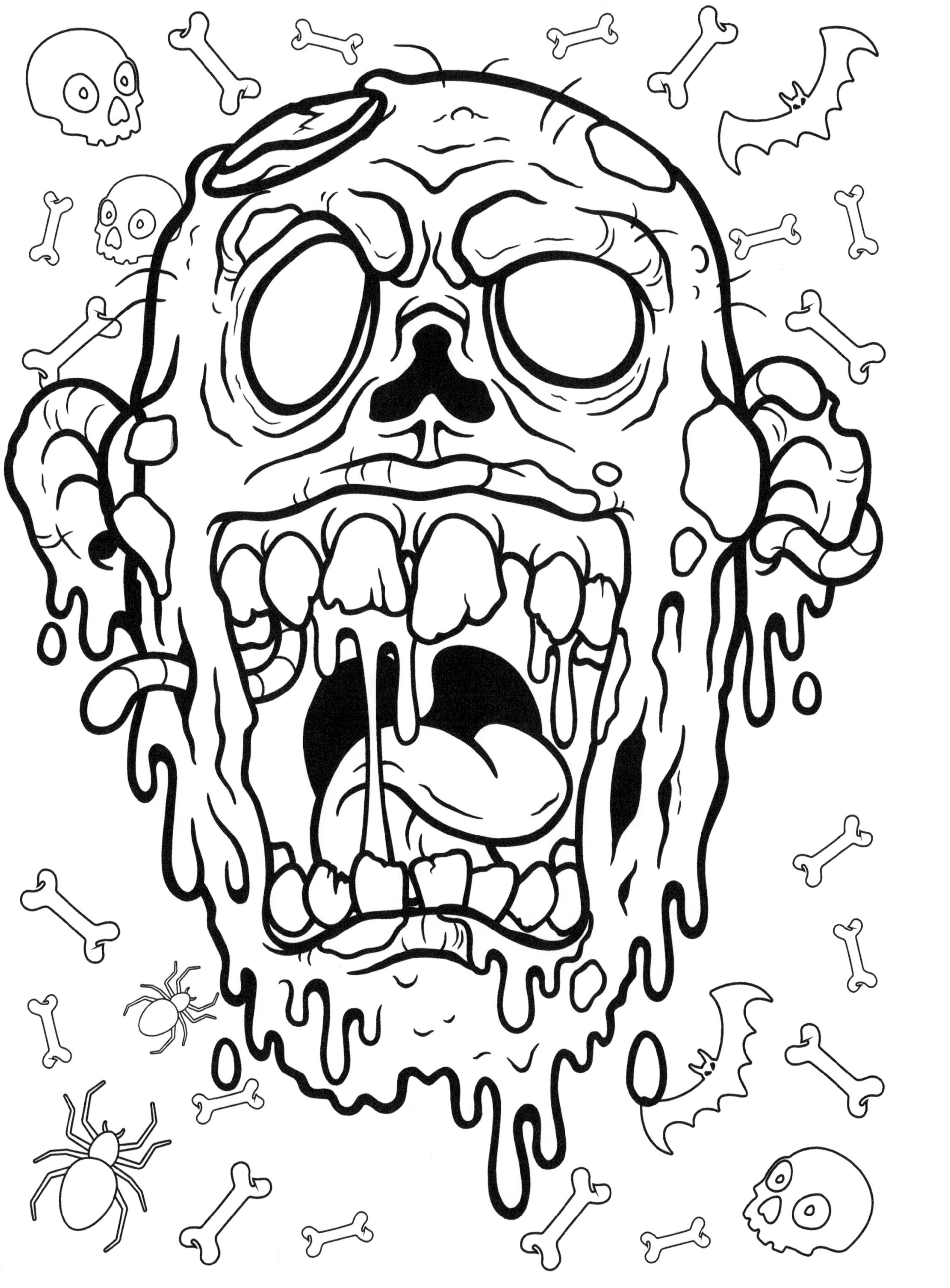

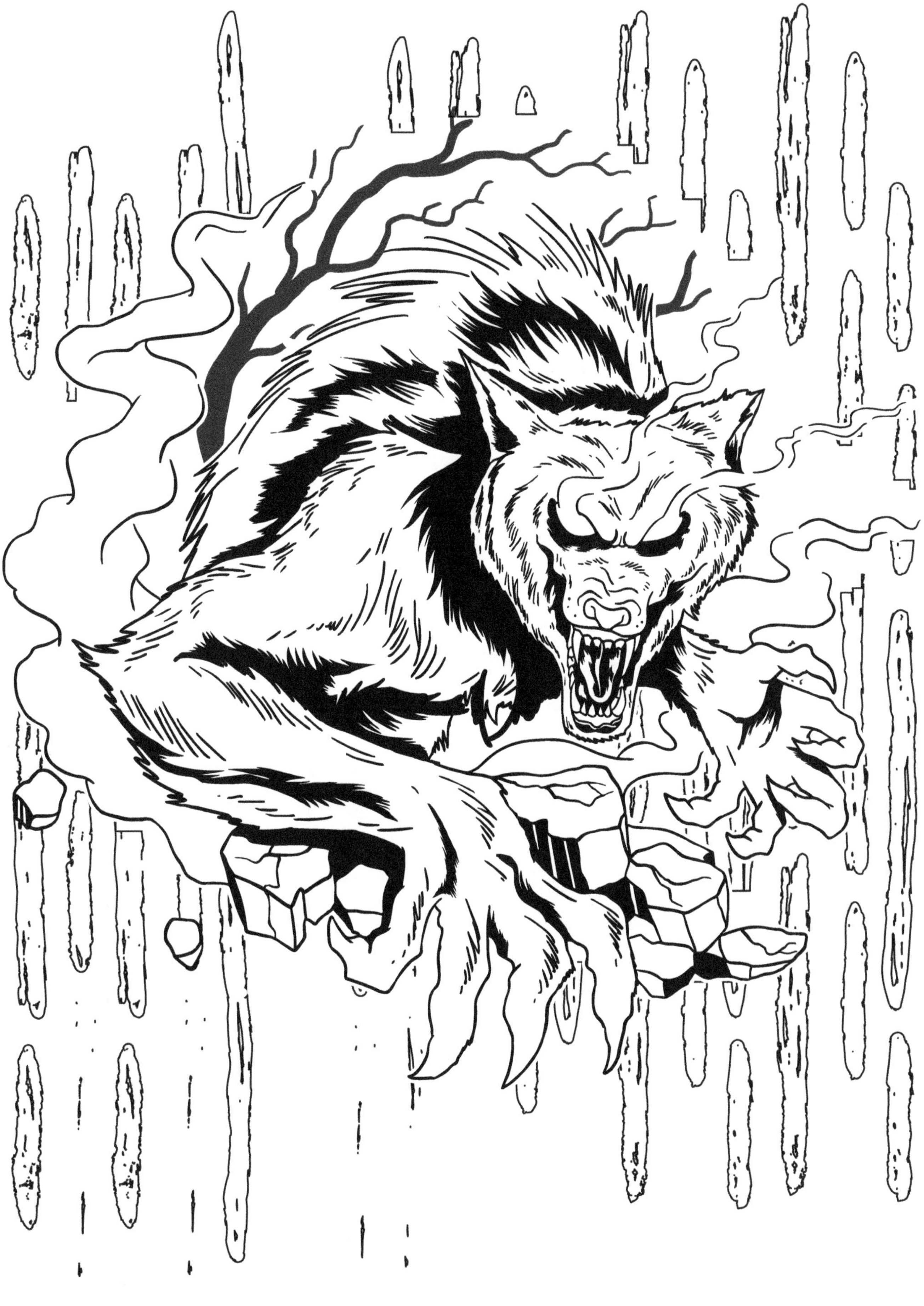

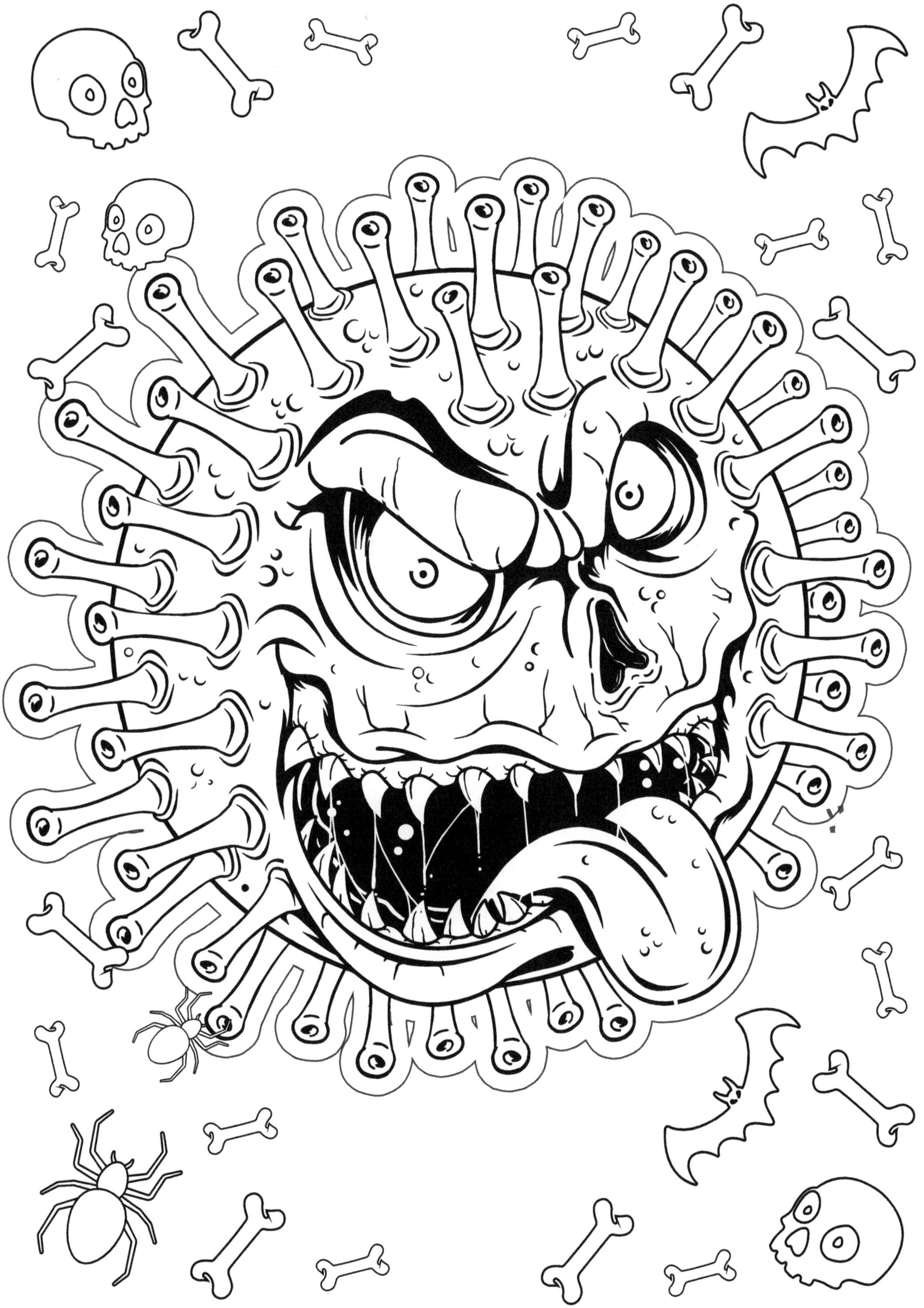

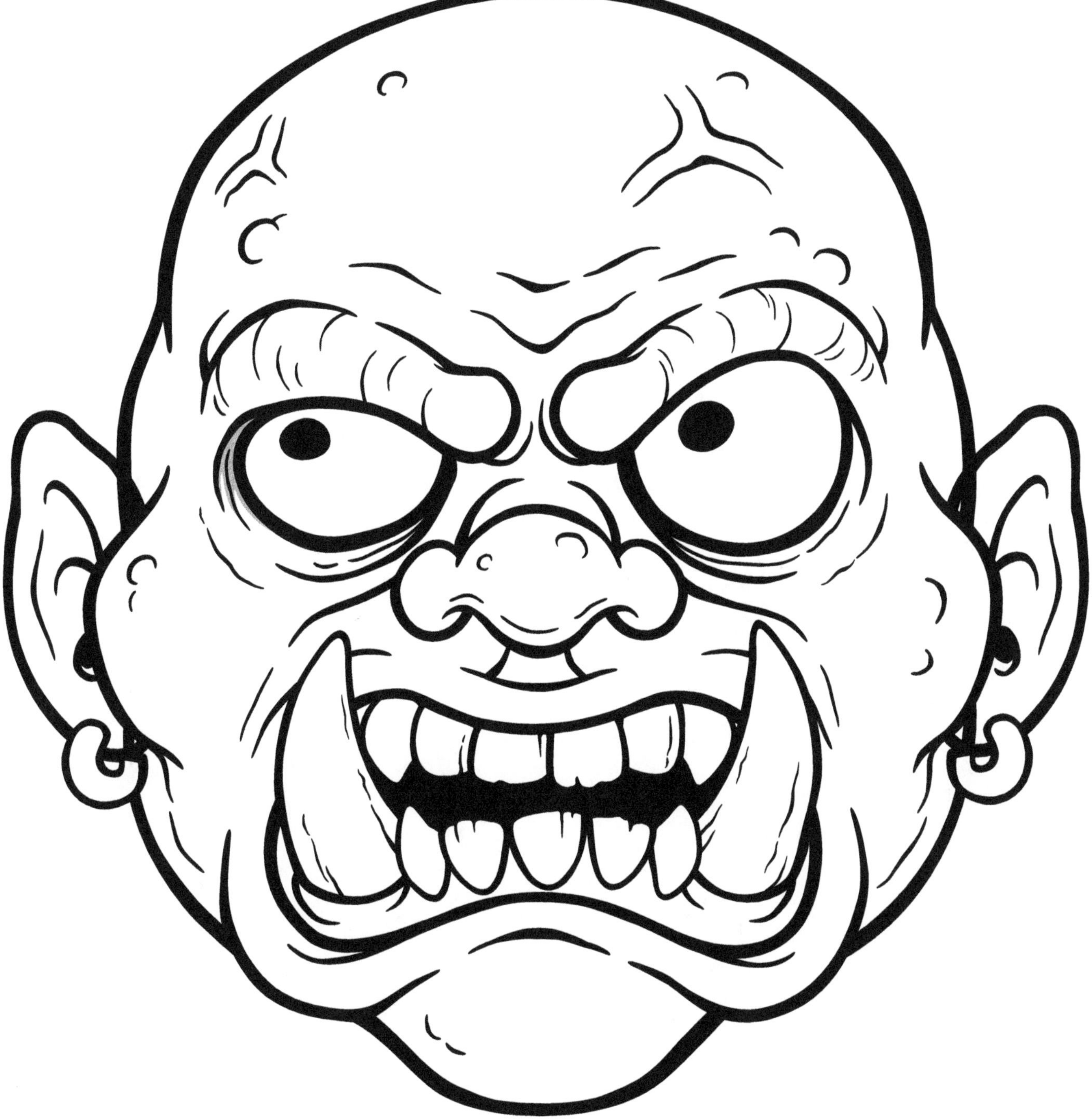

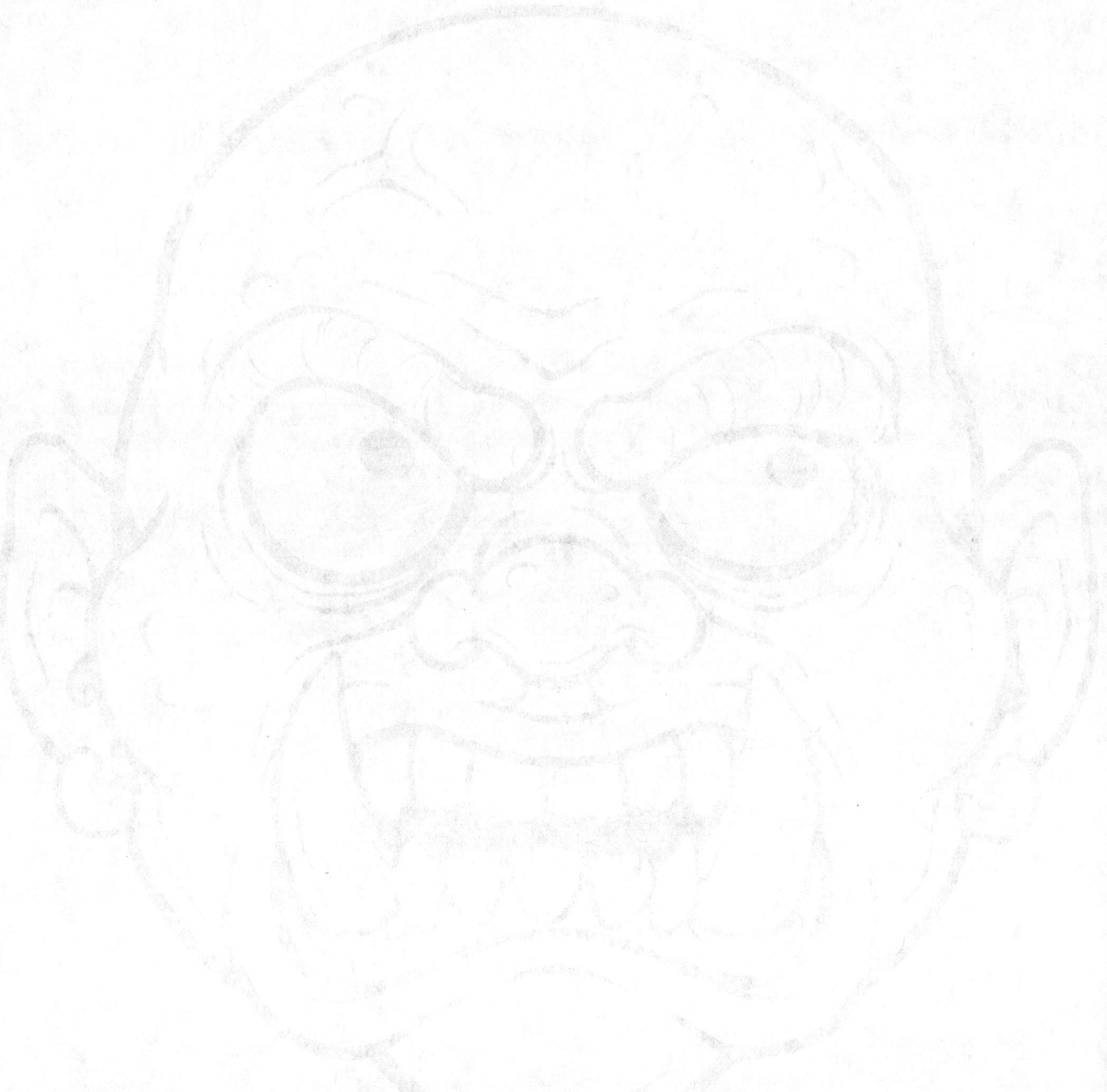

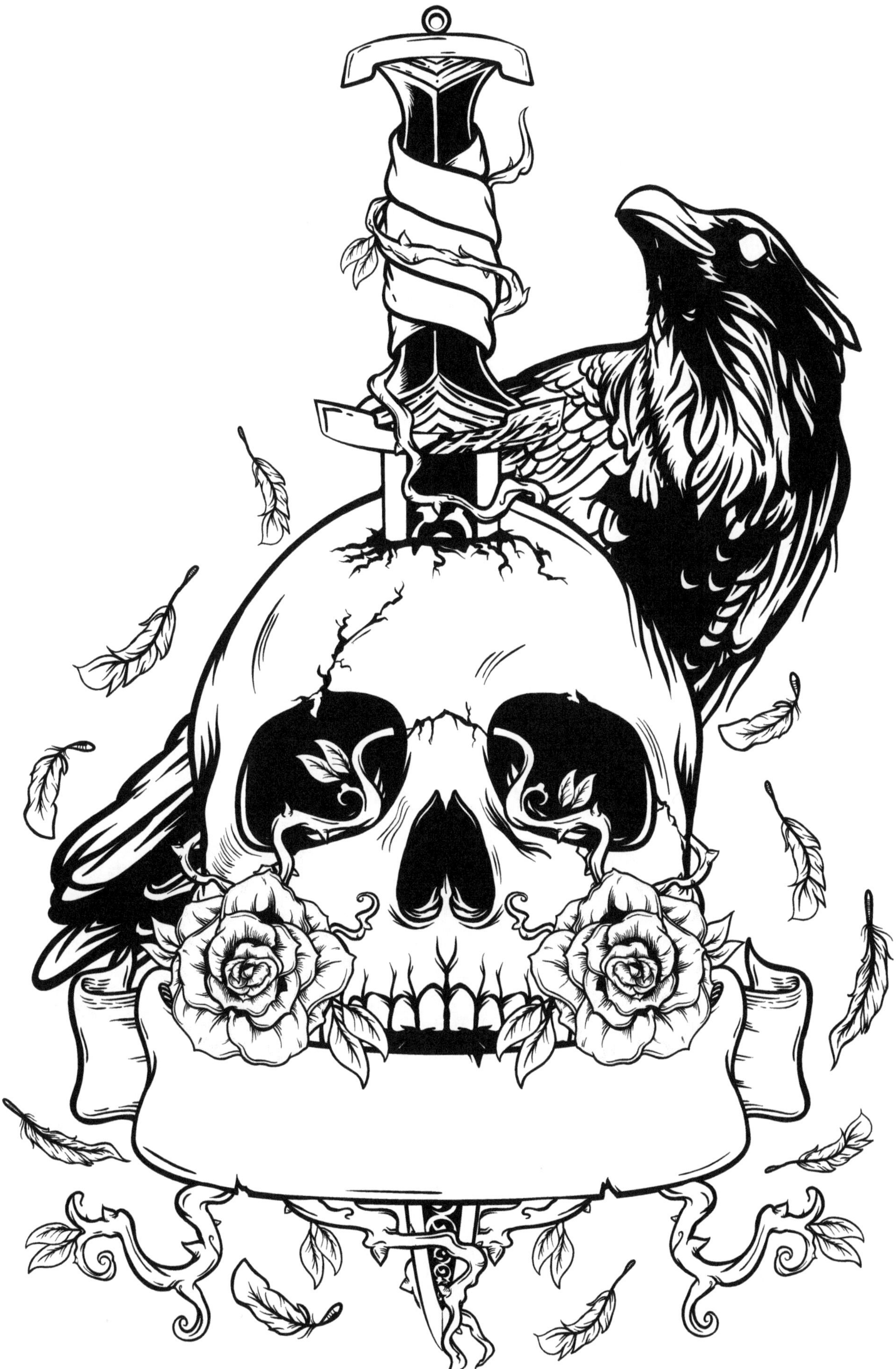

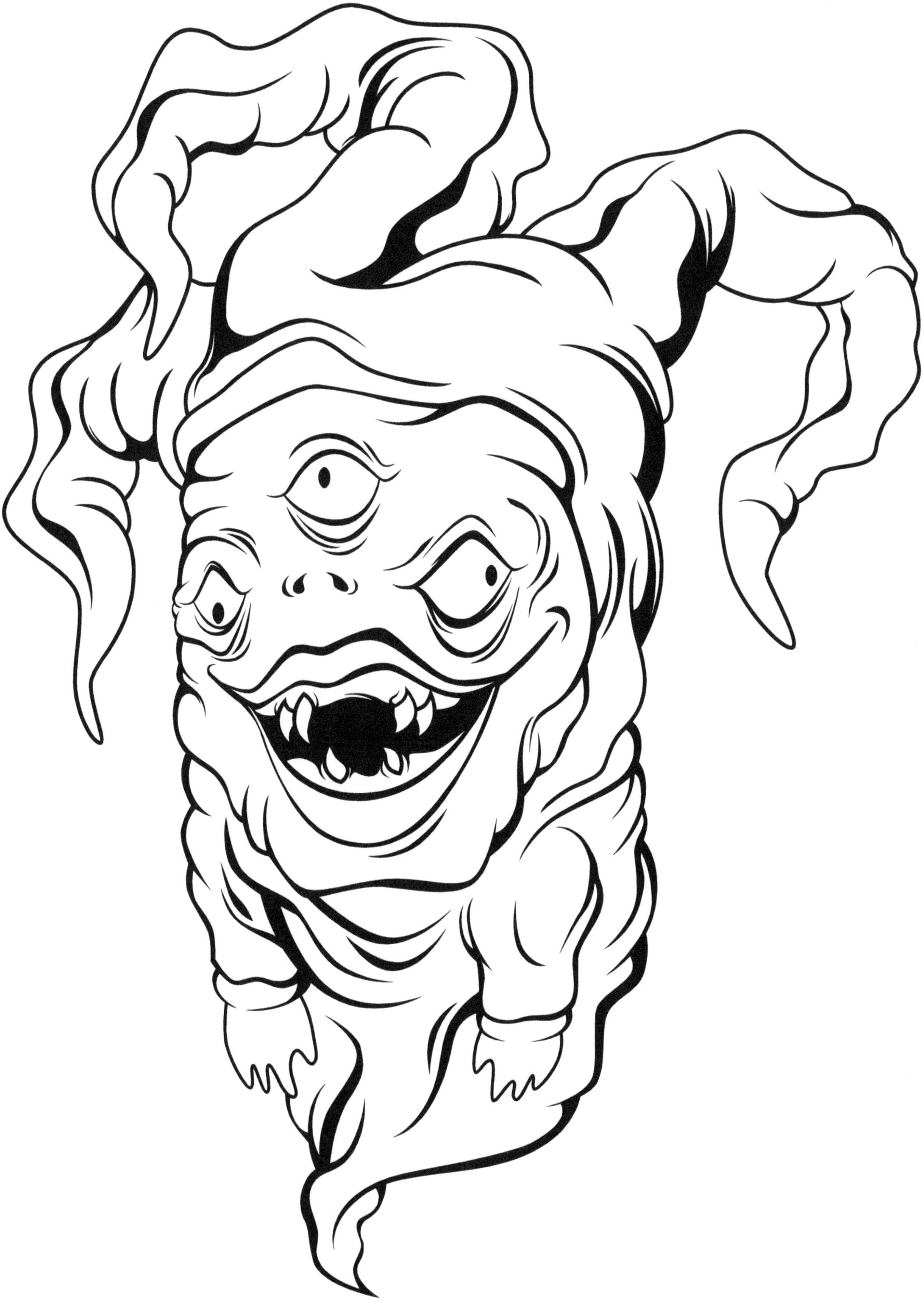

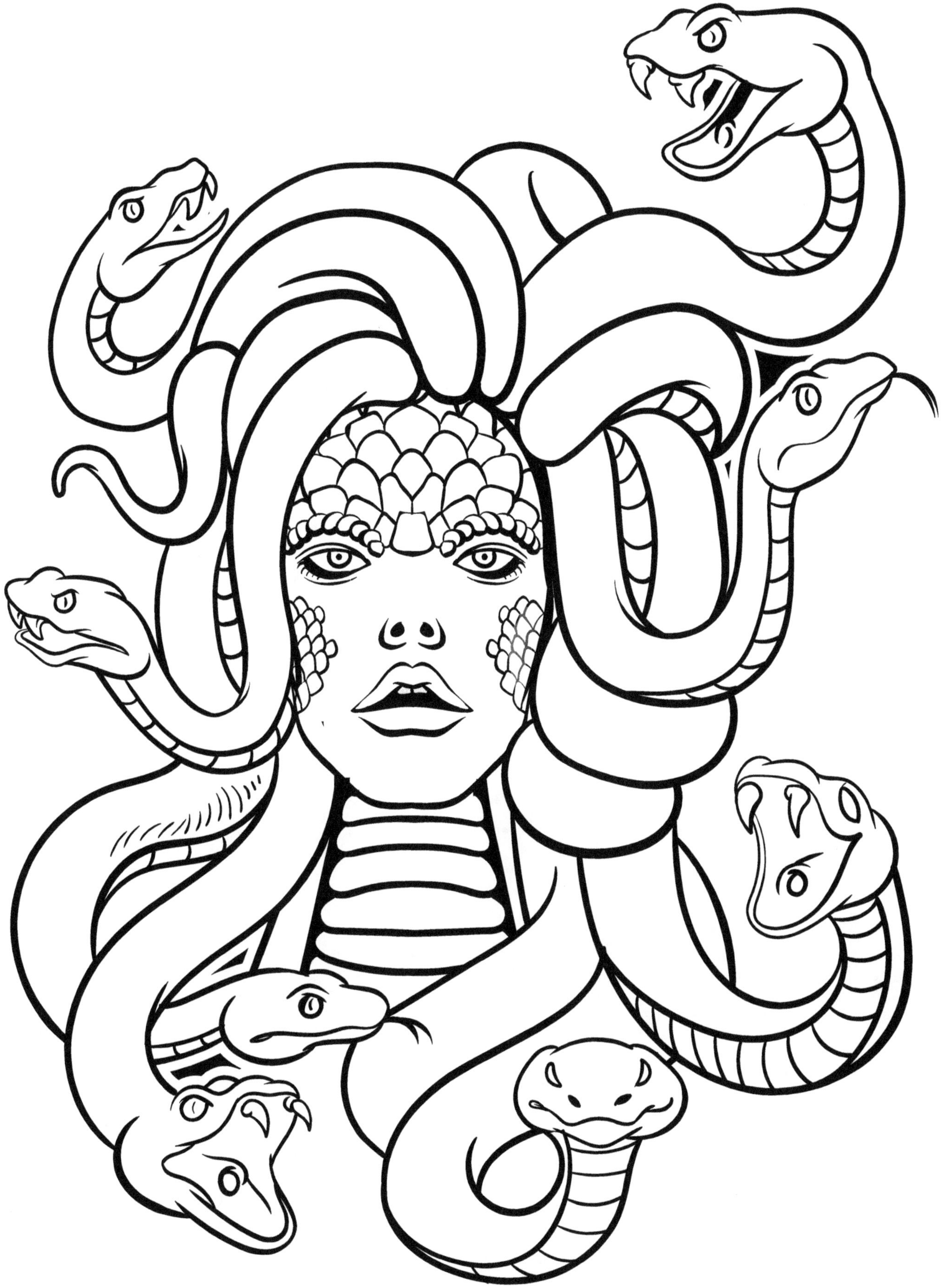

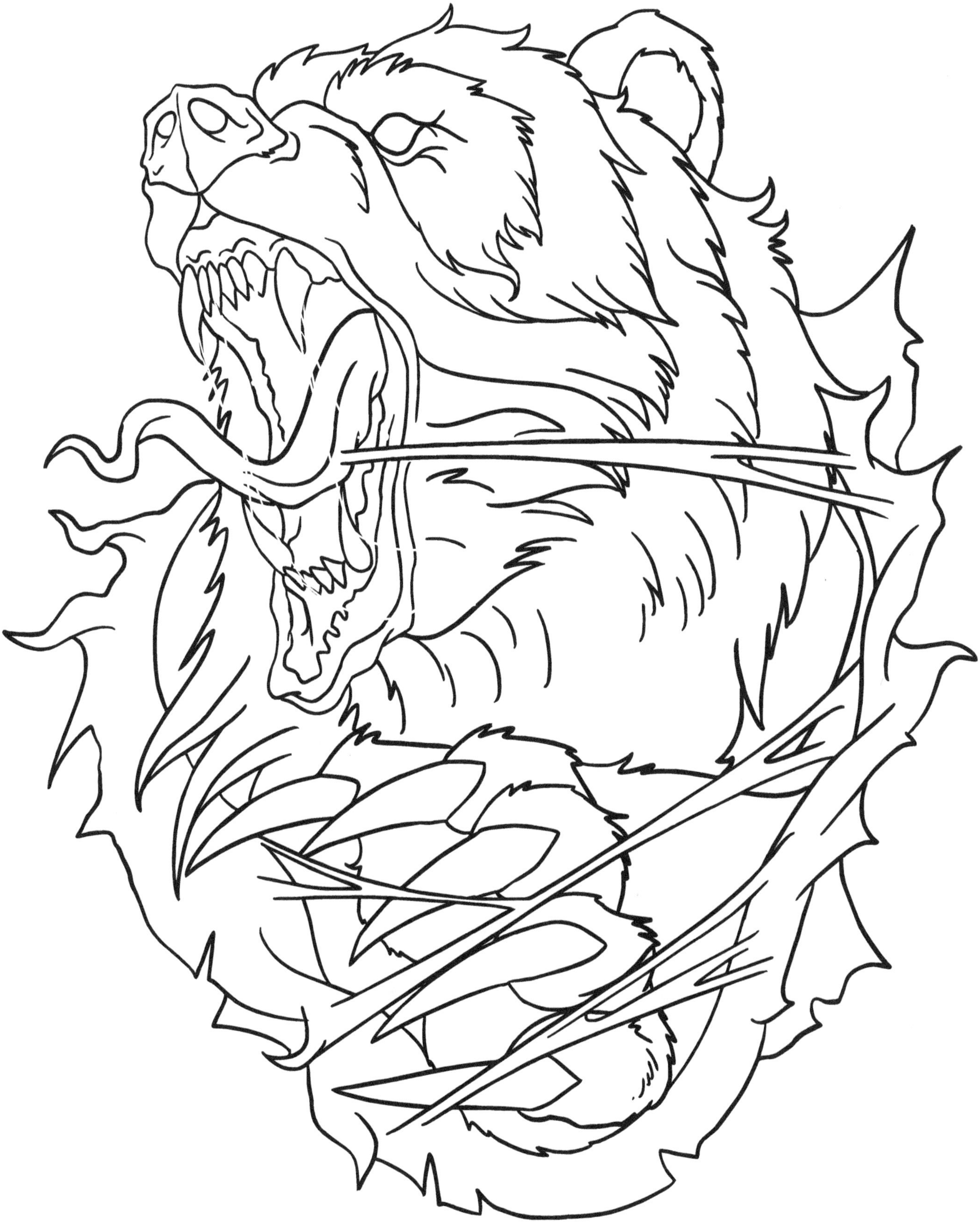

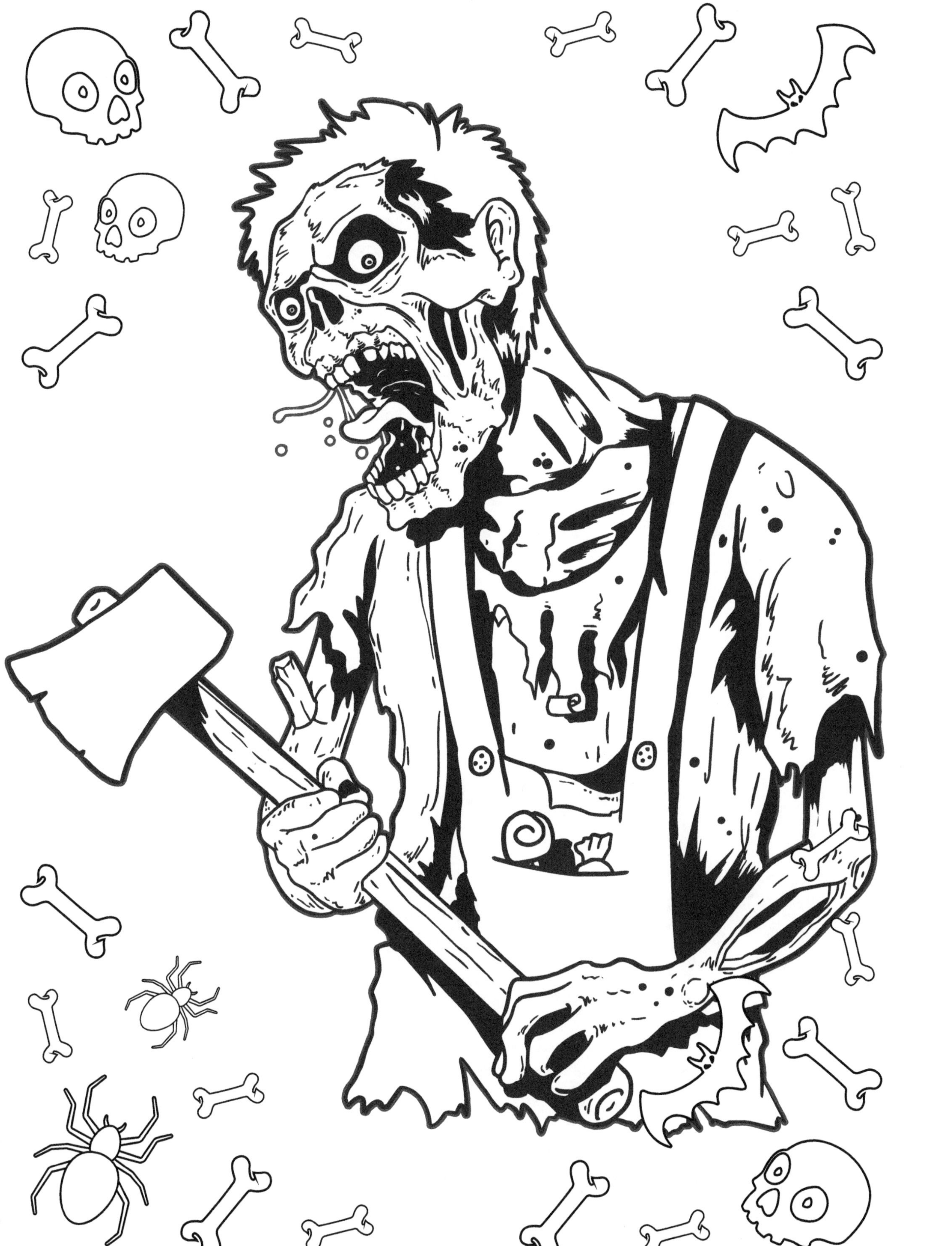

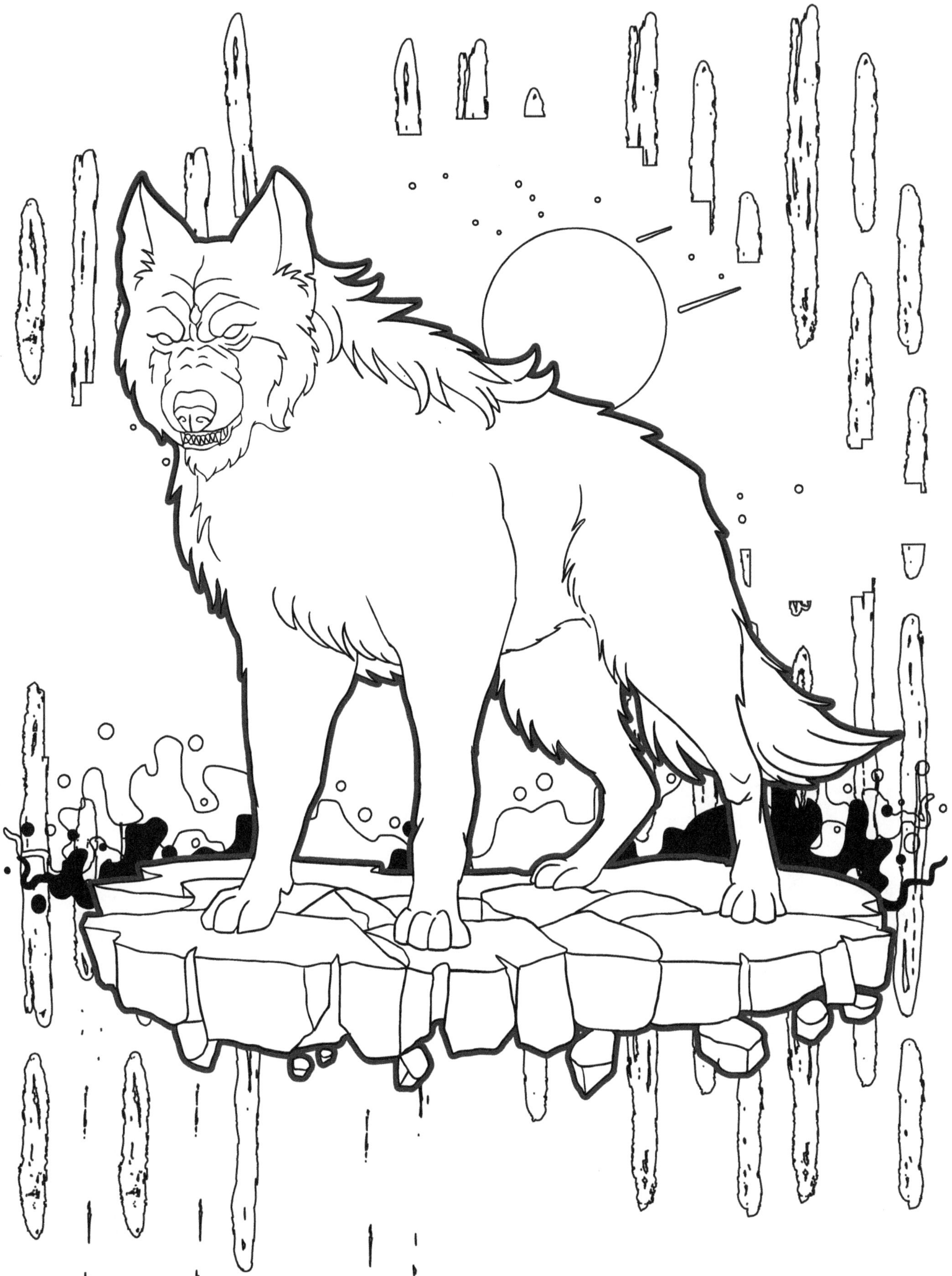

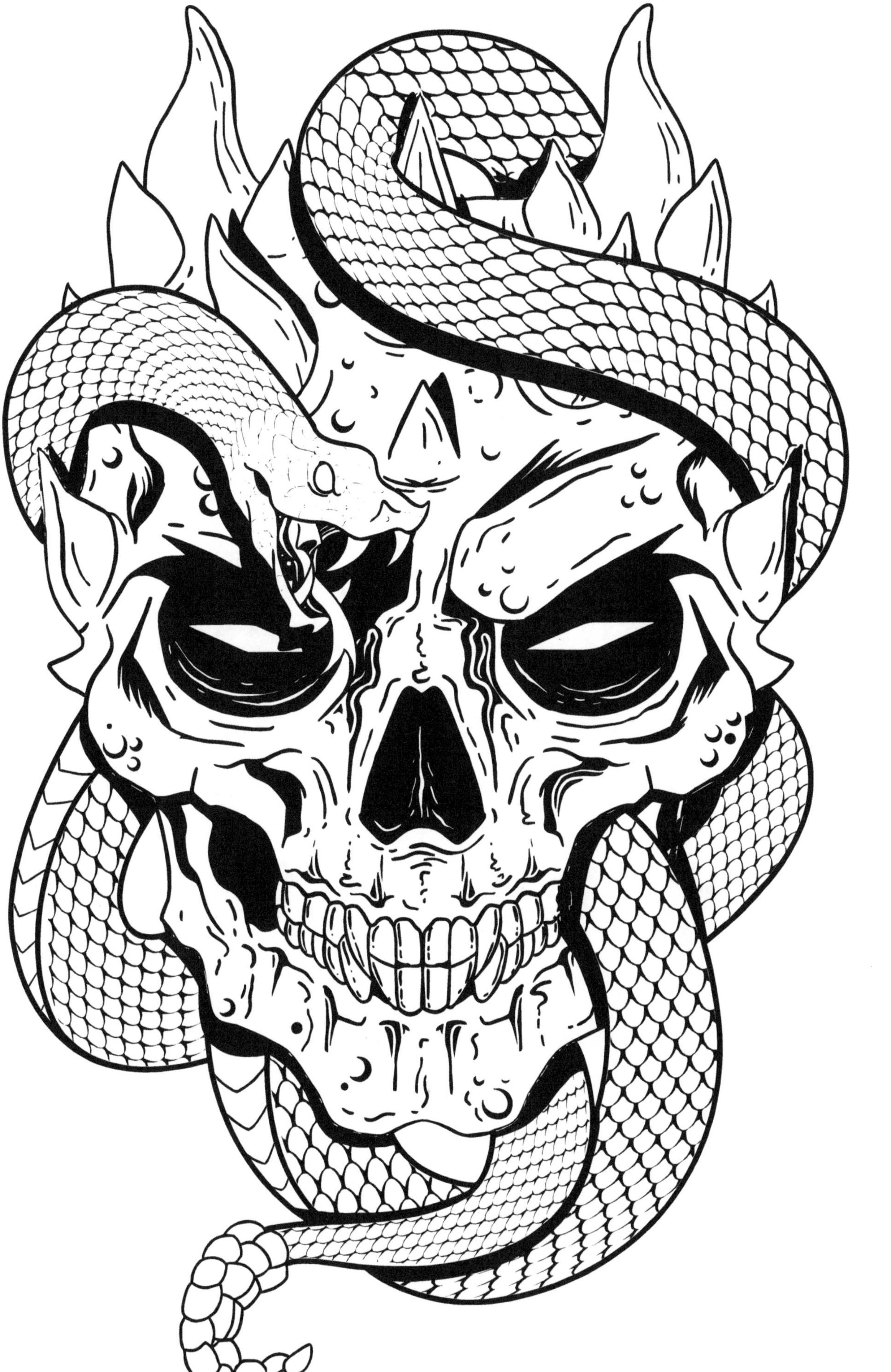

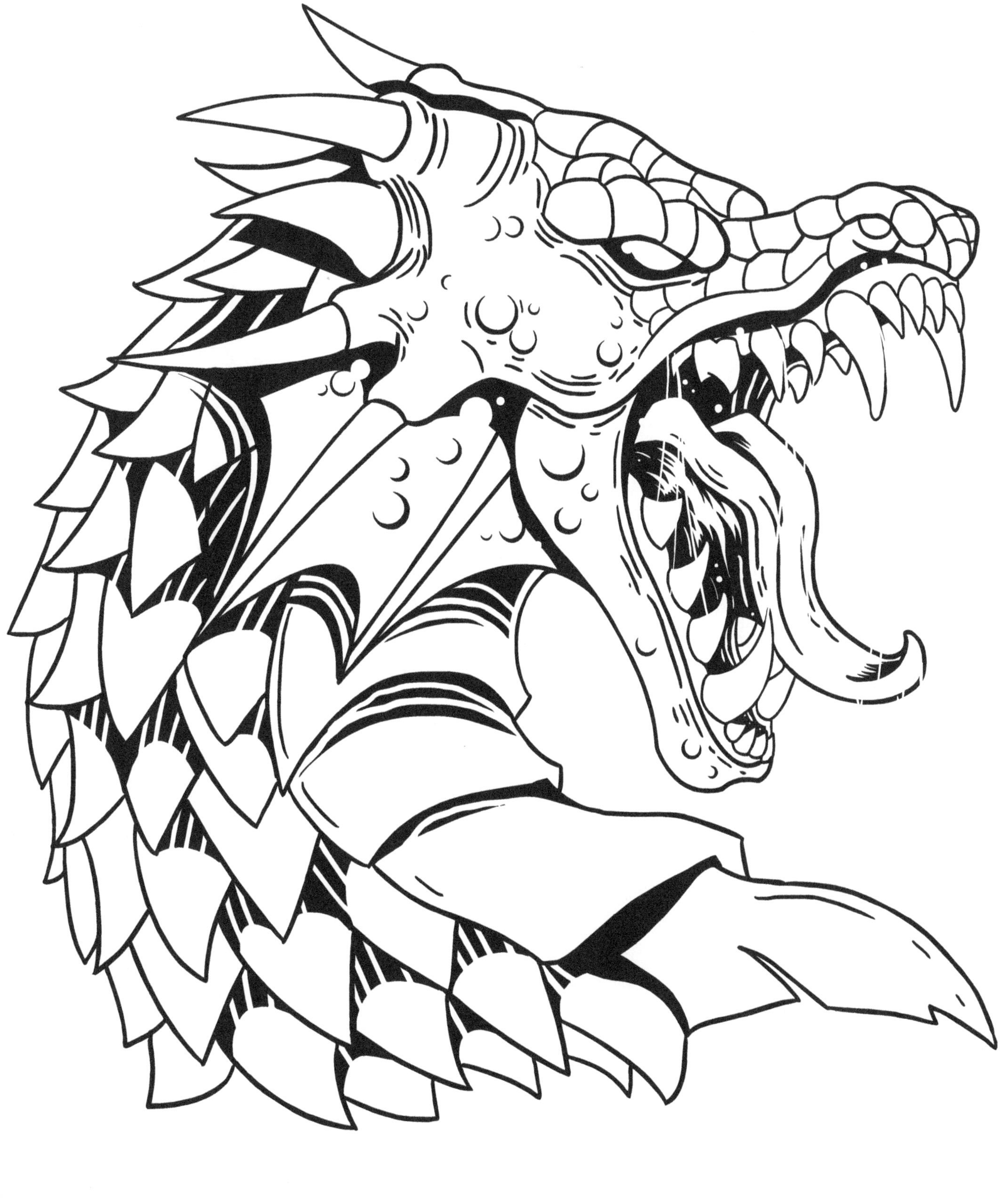

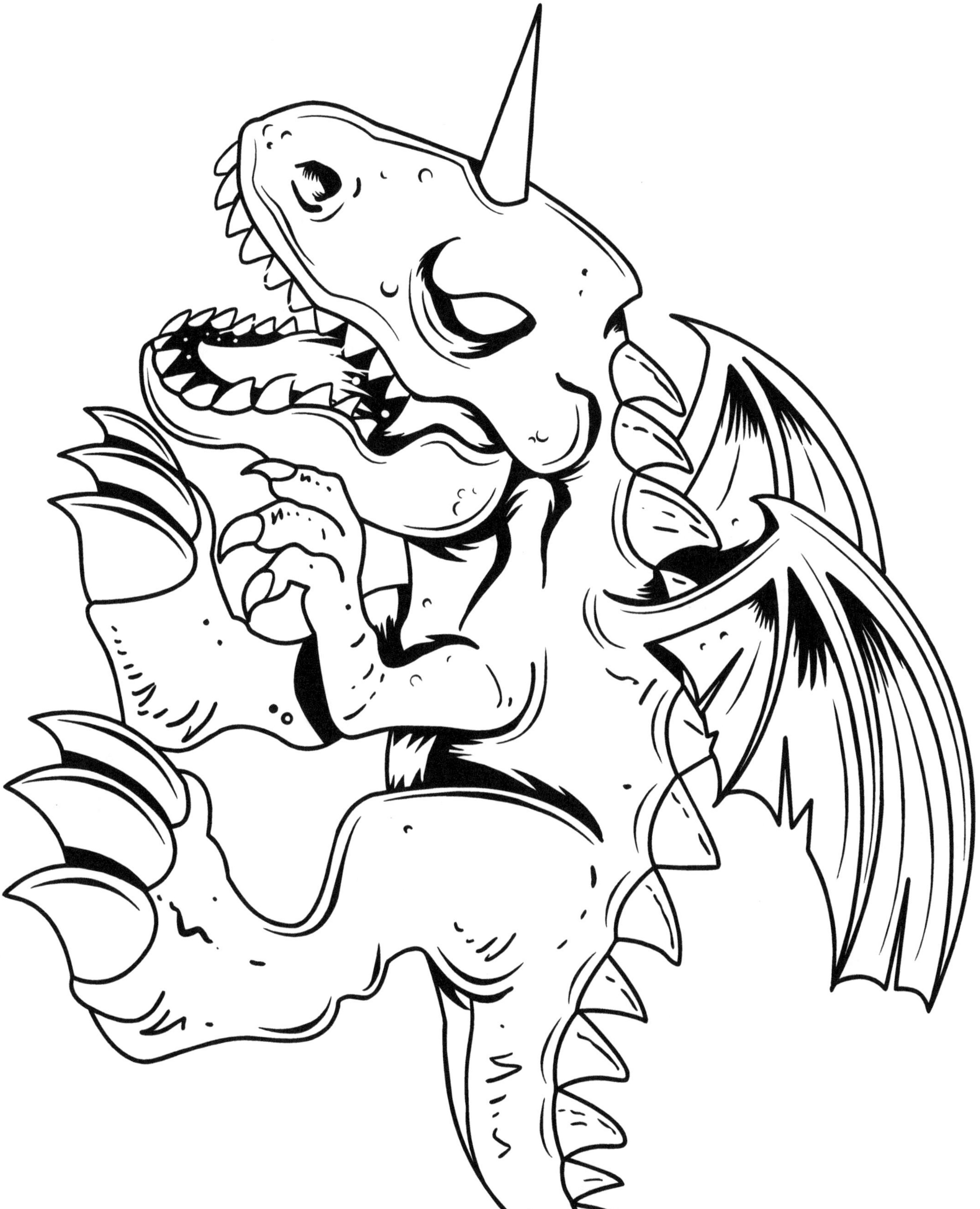

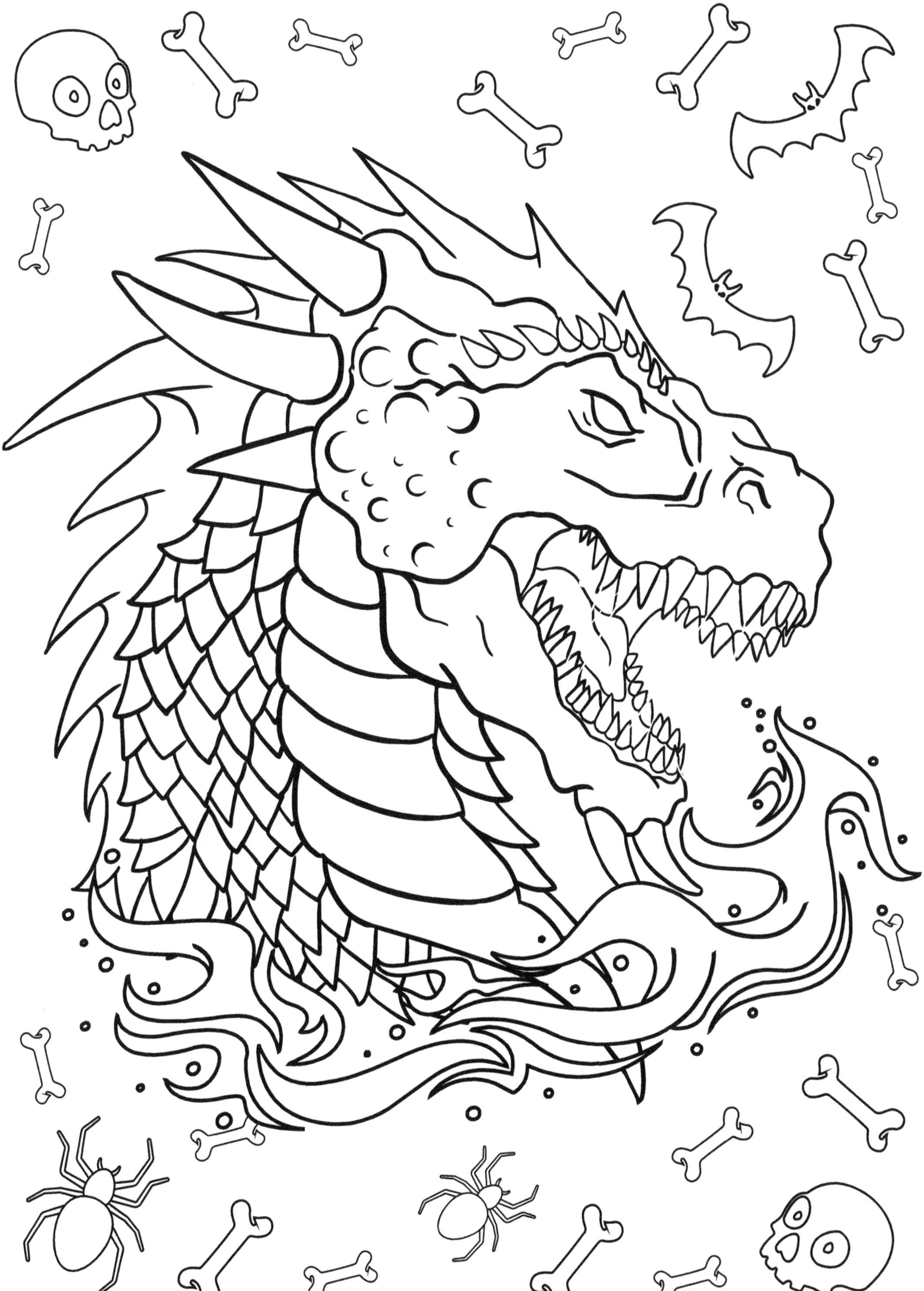

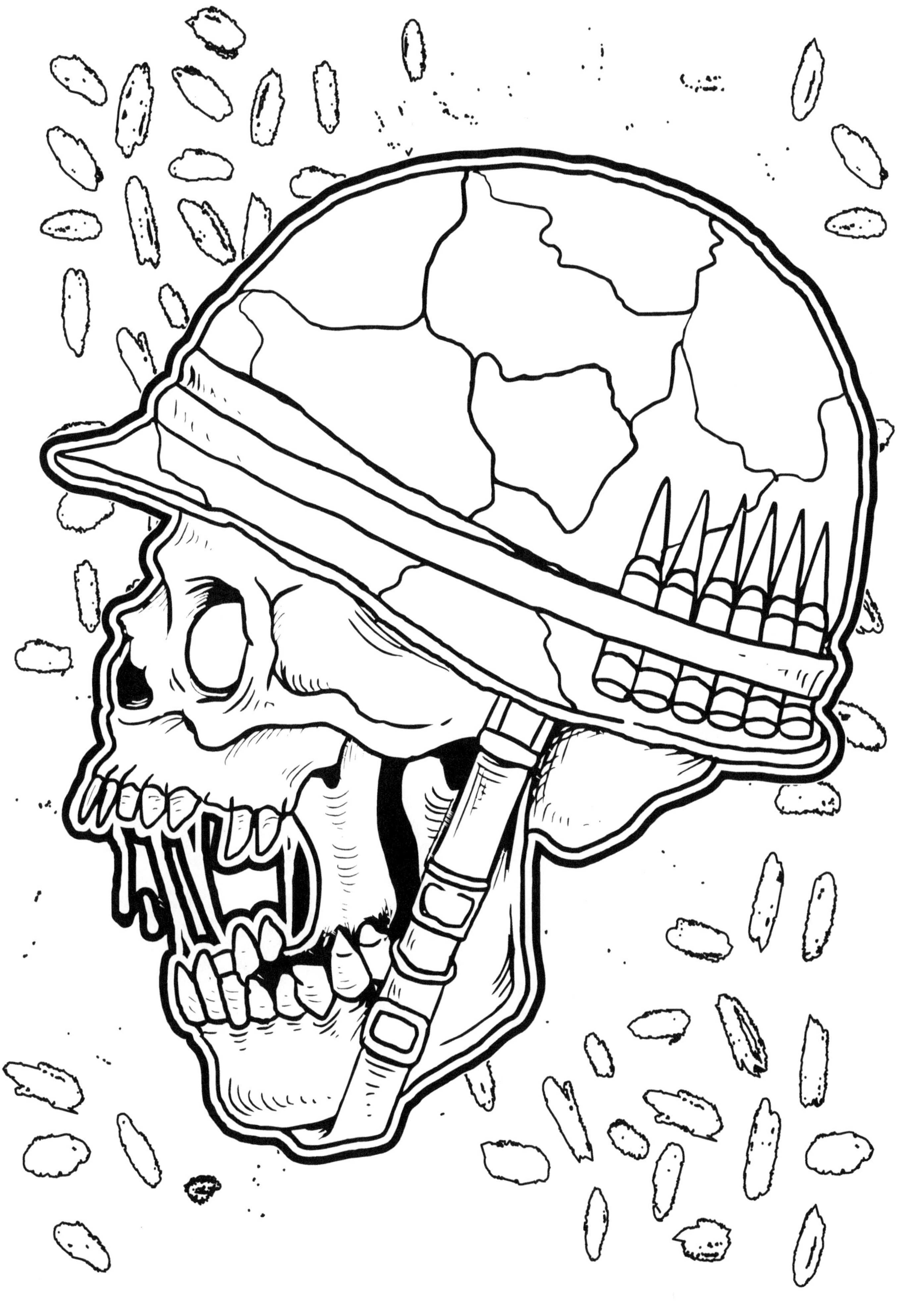

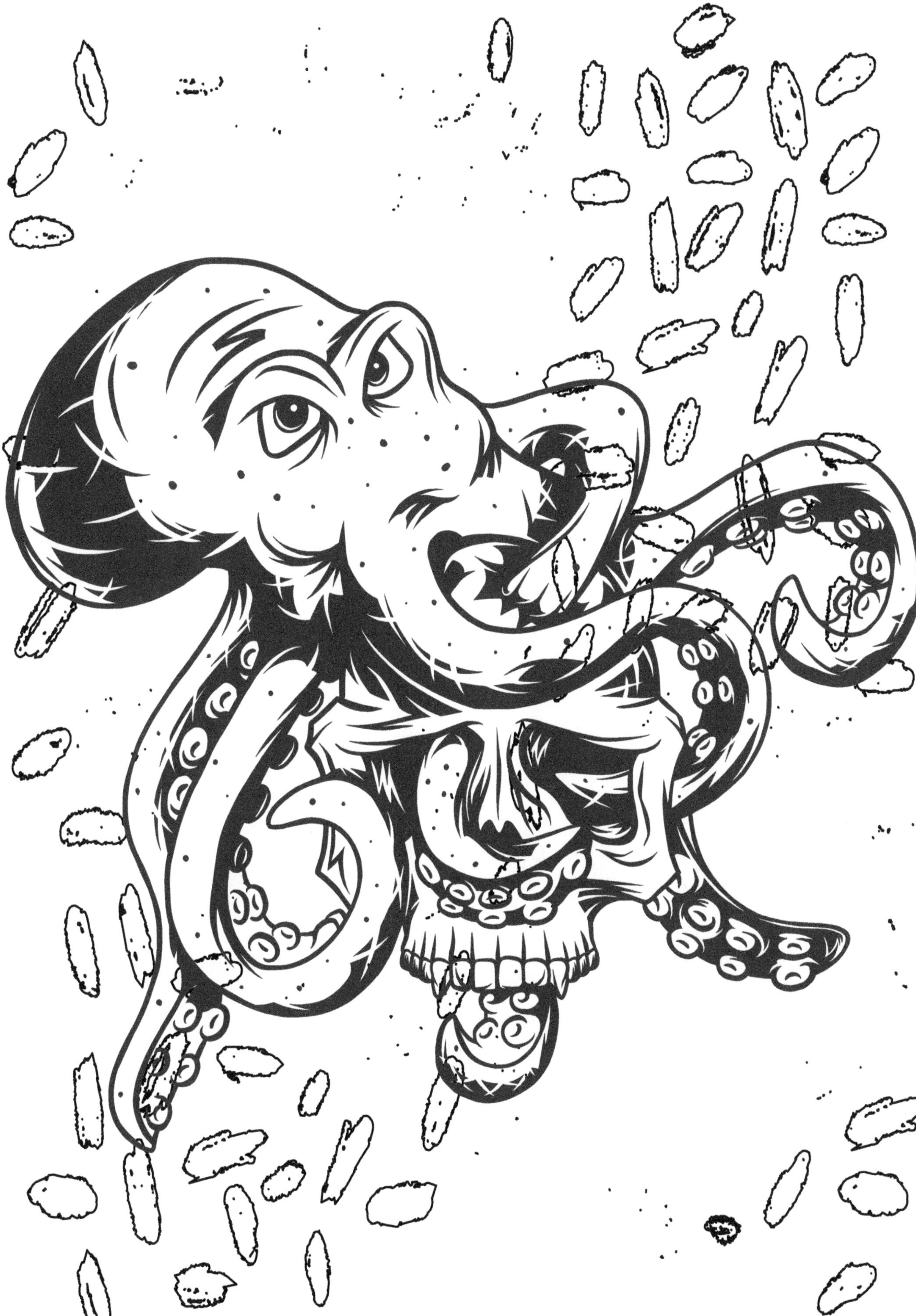

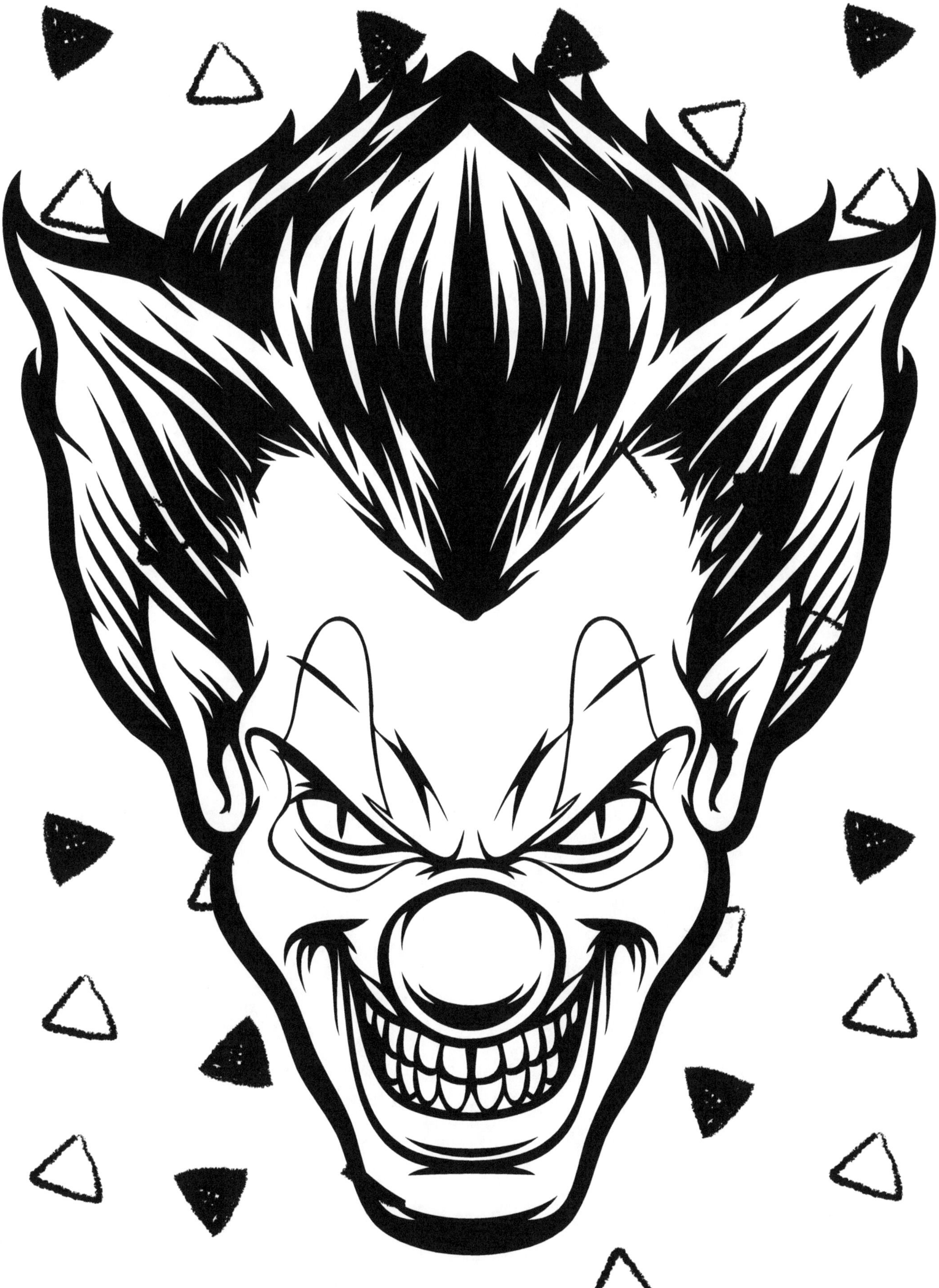

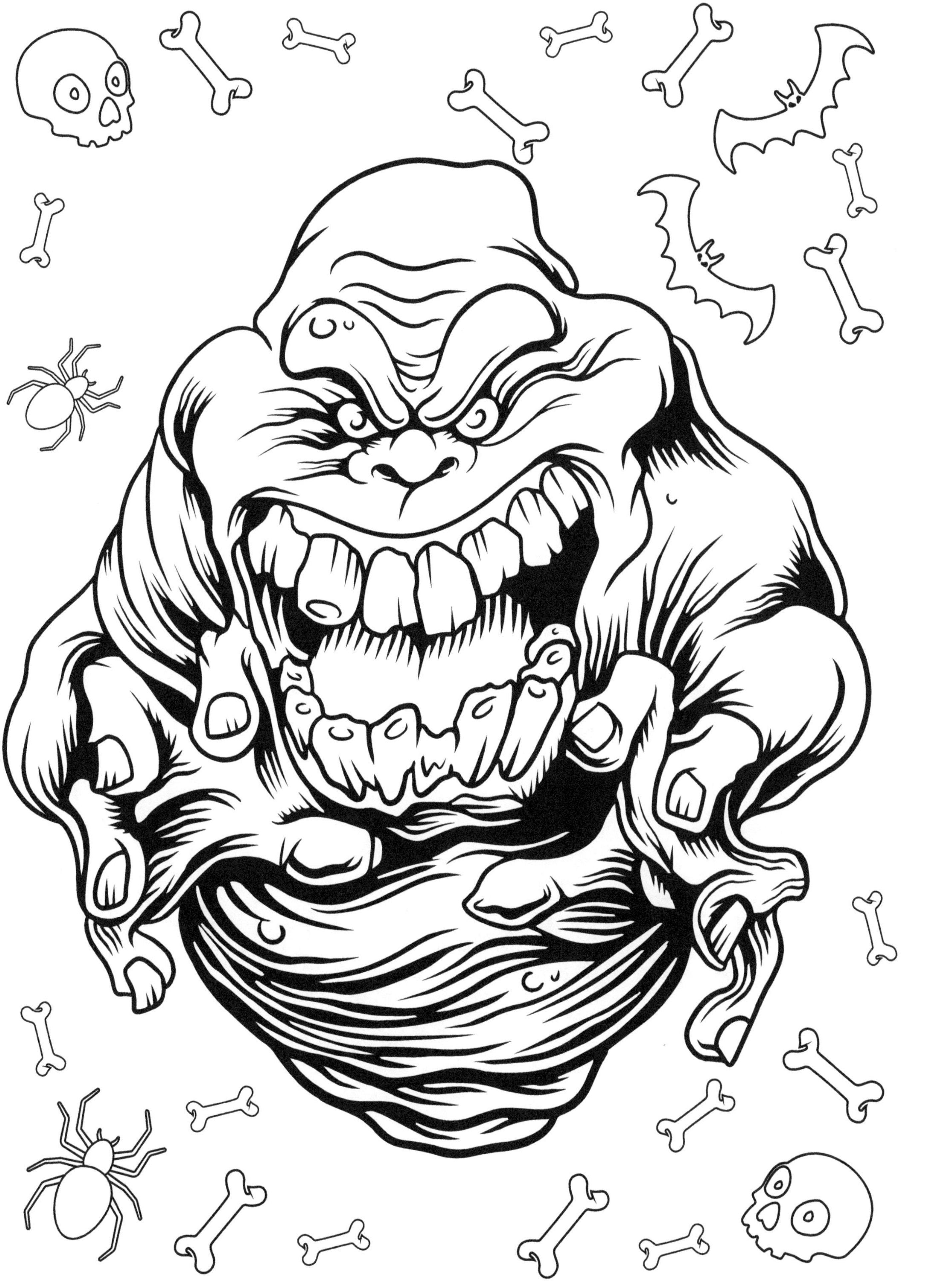

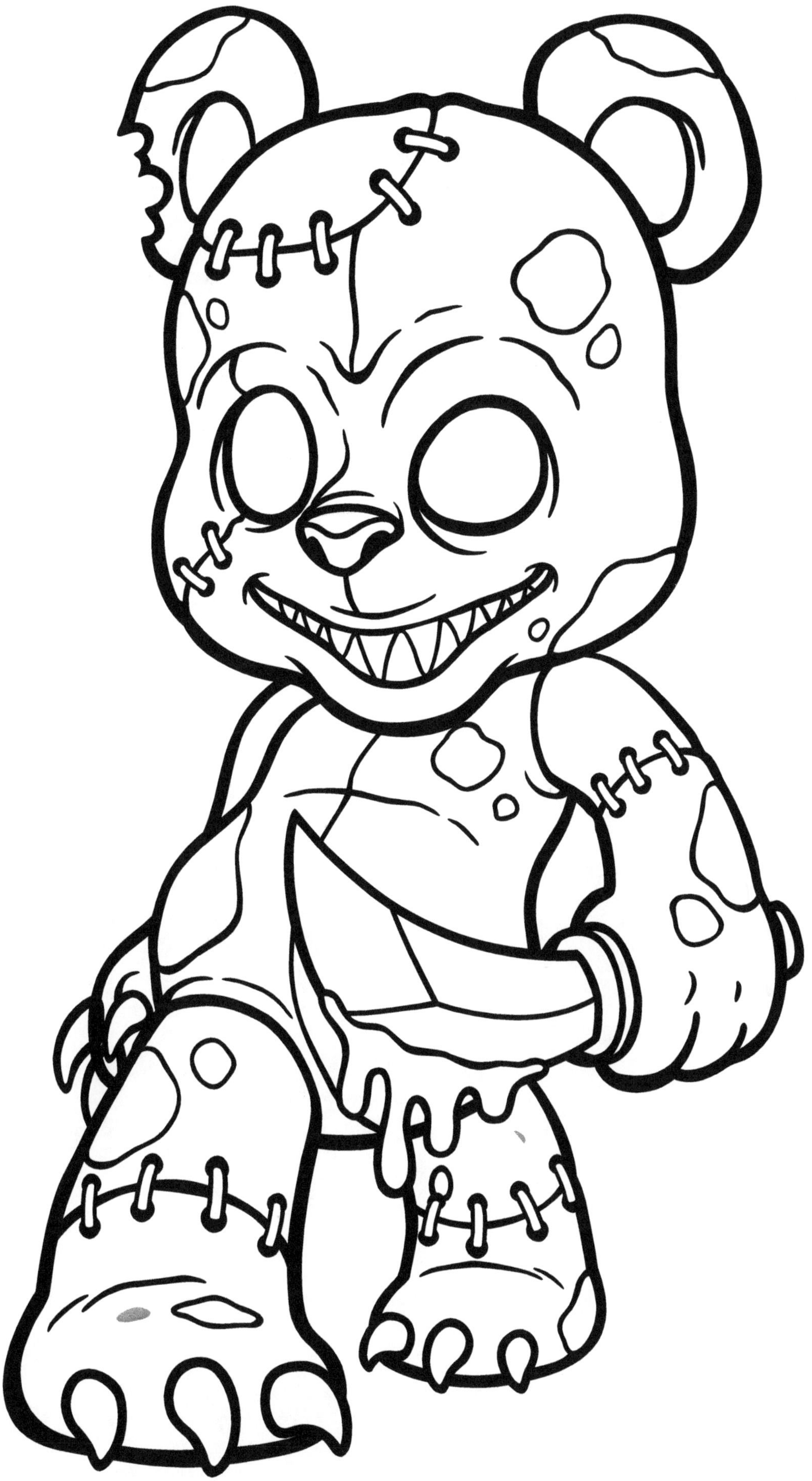

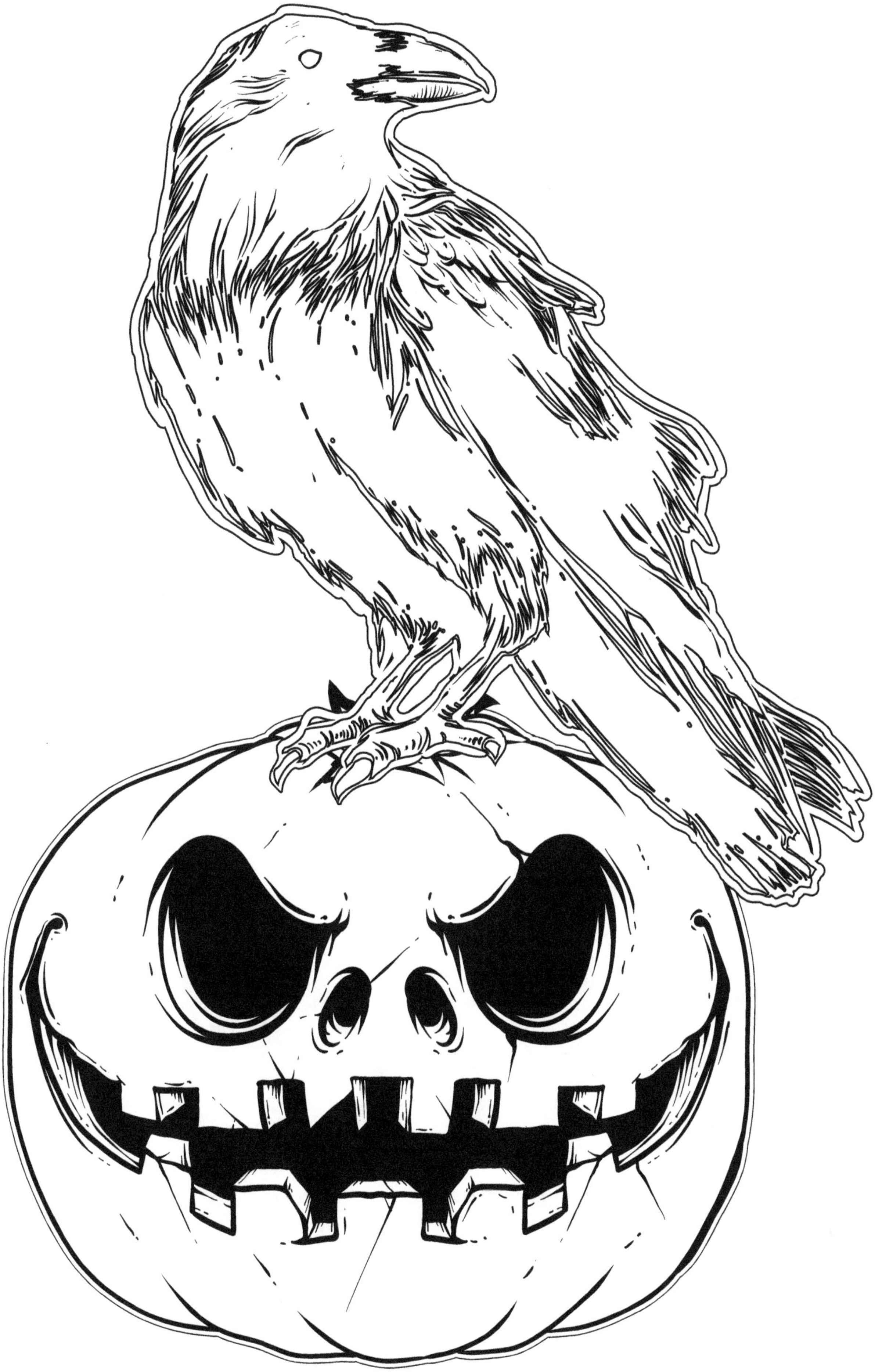

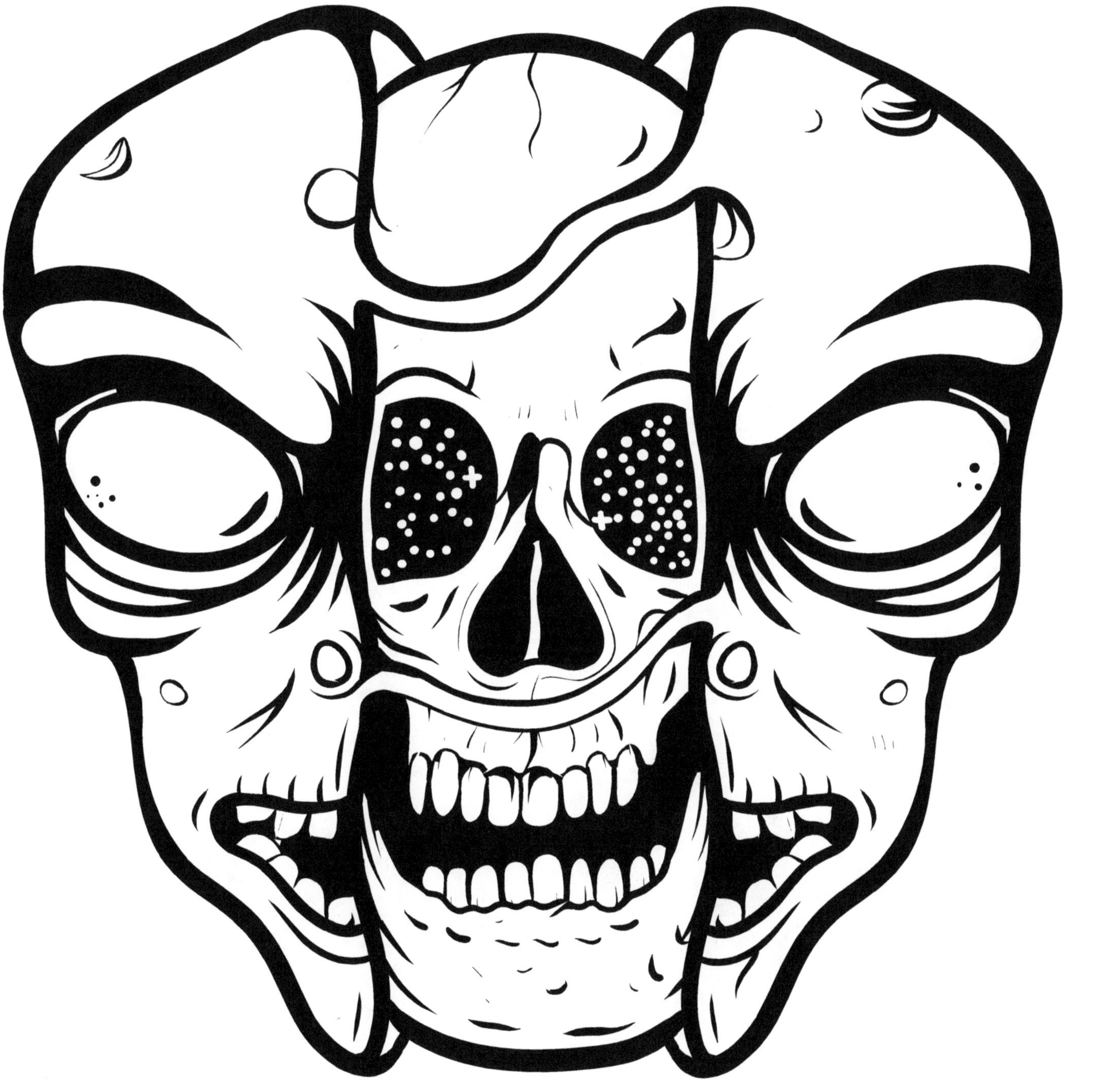

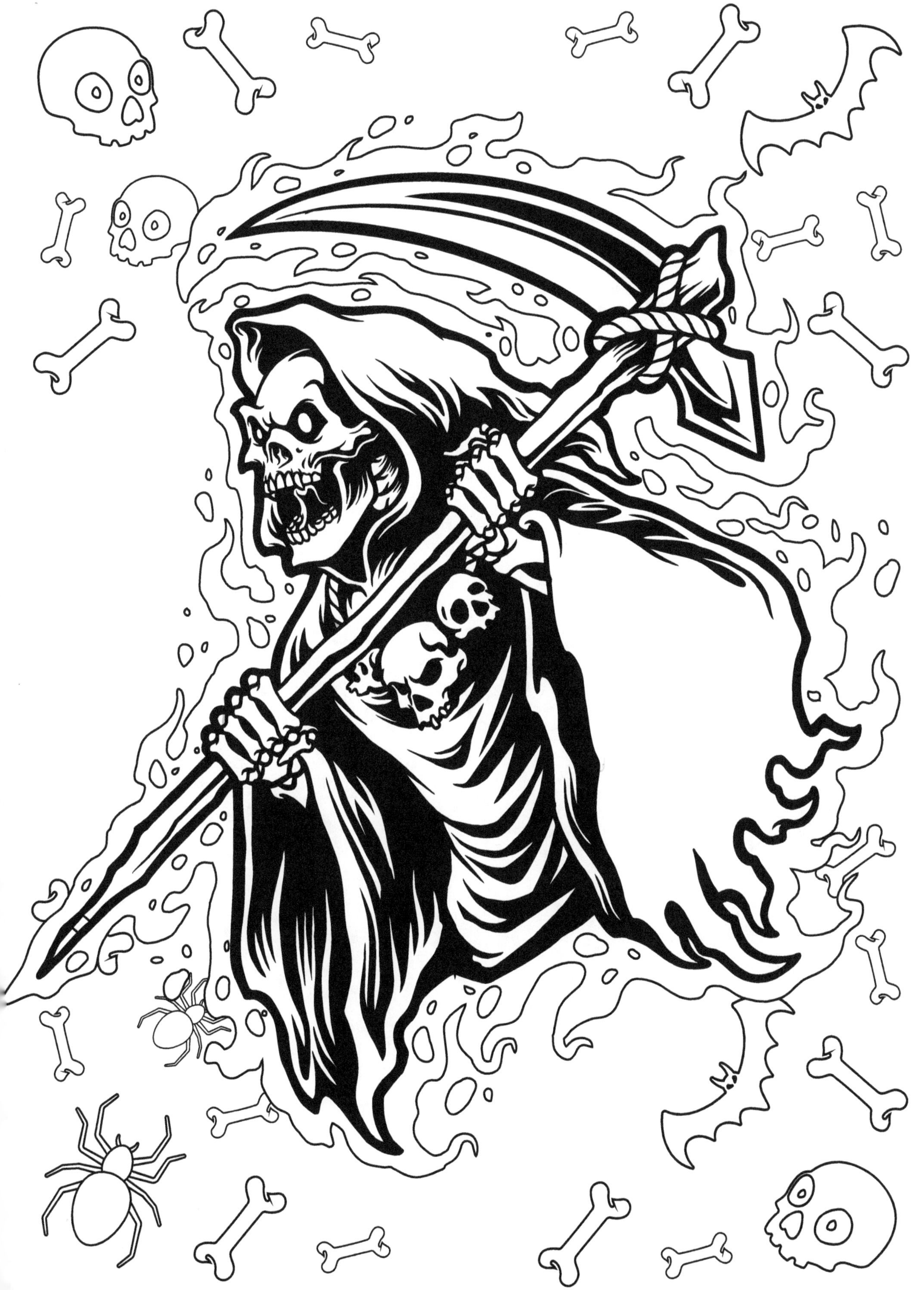

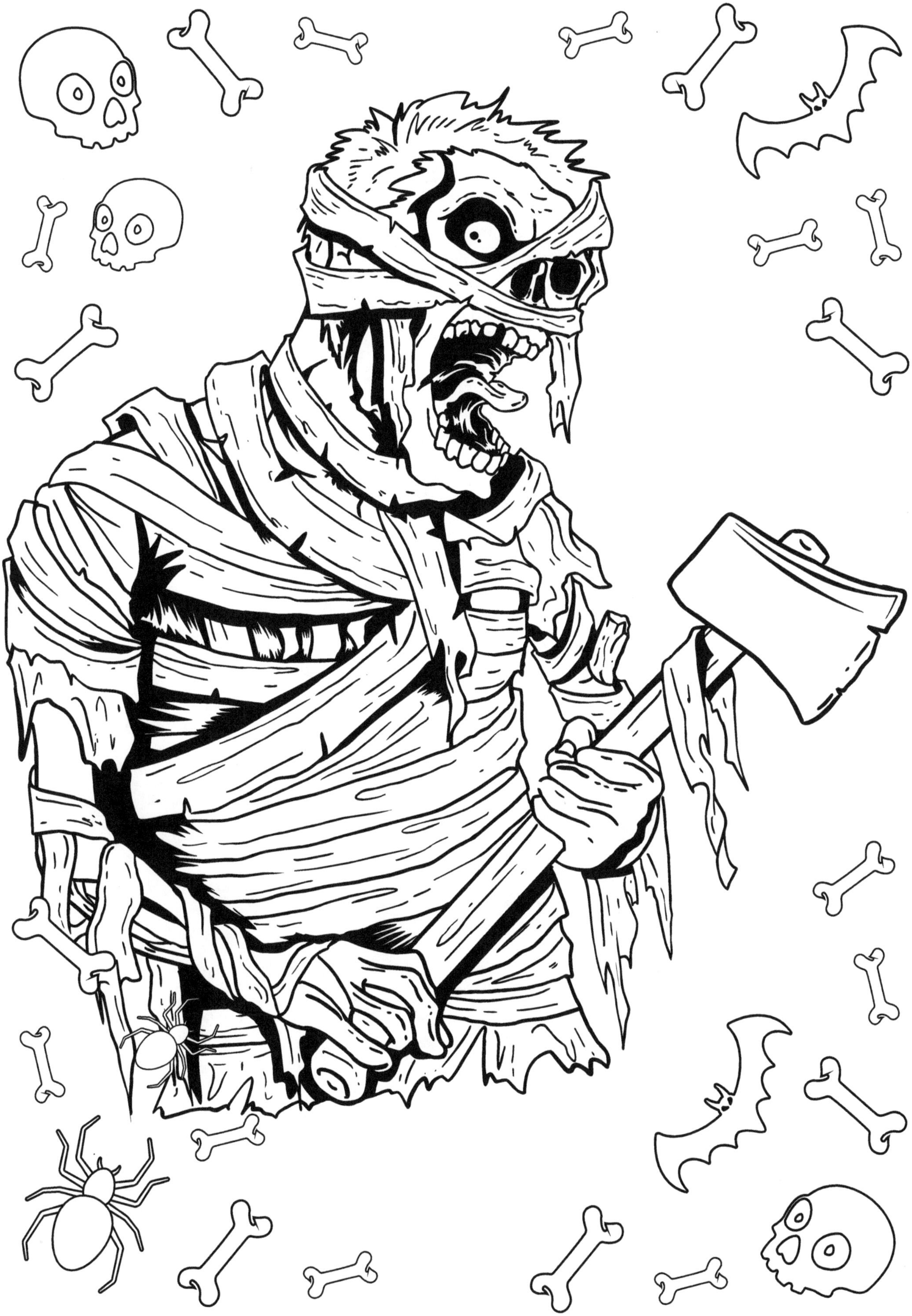

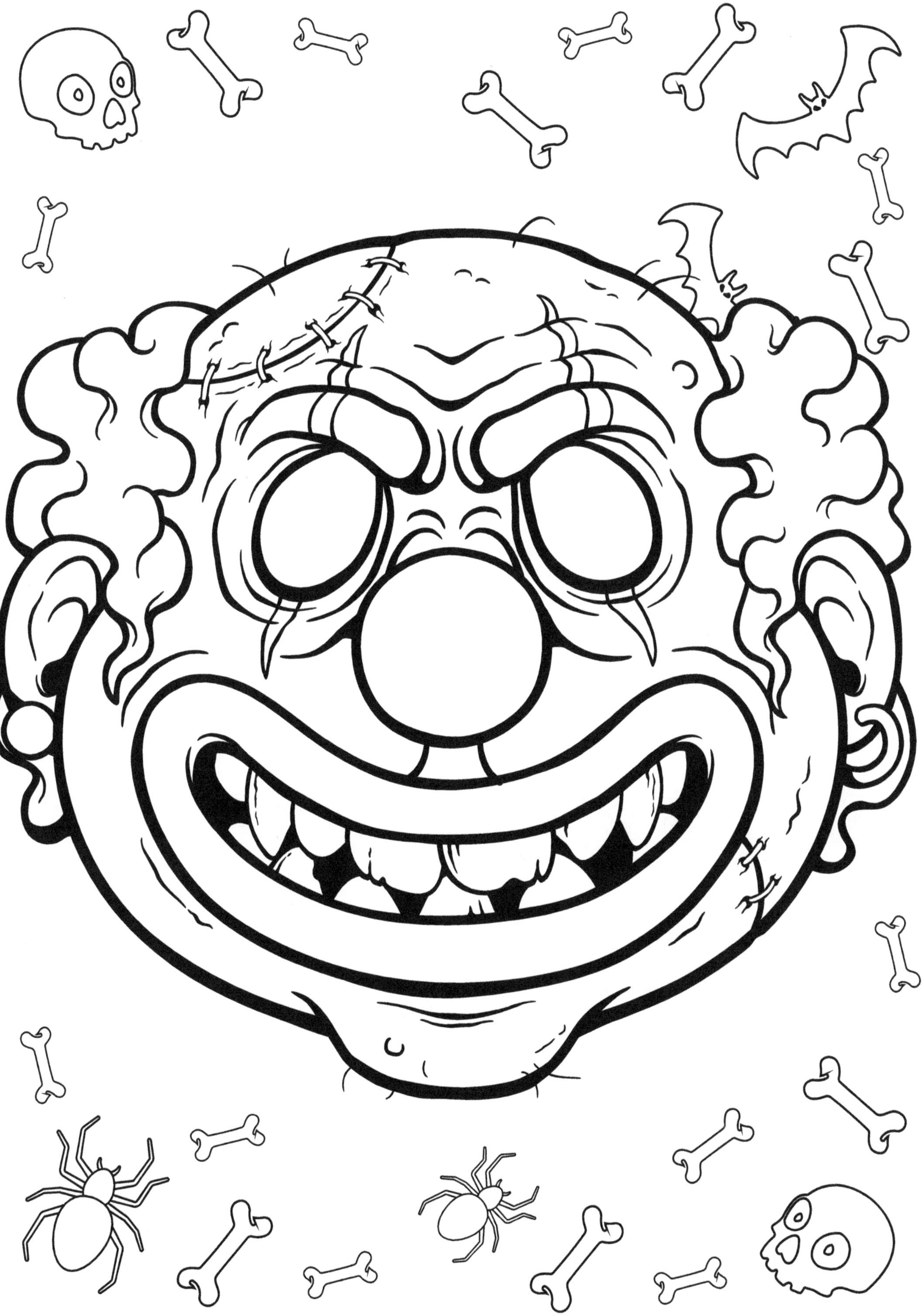

Printed in the USA
CPSIA information can be obtained
at www.ICGtesting.com
CBHW082153281124
18162CB00012B/517